Women, Freedom, and Calvin

Women, Freedom, and Calvin

Jane Dempsey Douglass

The 1983 Annie Kinkead Warfield Lectures

The Westminster Press
Philadelphia

Grateful acknowledgment is made to the original publishers for permission to use material previously included in the following publications:

The American Society of Church History: Jane Dempsey Douglass, "Christian Freedom: What Calvin Learned at the School of Women," *Church History* 53 (June 1984), pp. 155–173.

Princeton Theological Seminary: Jane Dempsey Douglass, "Christian Freedom in Calvin's Theology," *The Princeton Seminary Bulletin*, vol. IV, no. 2 (1983), pp. 69–83.

Simon & Schuster: Jane Dempsey Douglass, "Women and the Continental Reformation," in *Religion and Sexism: Images of Woman in the Jewish and Christian Traditions*, ed. Rosemary Radford Ruether (New York: Simon & Schuster, 1974).

The Westminster Press: *Calvin: Institutes of the Christian Religion*, ed. John T. McNeill, trans. Ford Lewis Battles, The Library of Christian Classics, vols. XX and XXI; copyright © MCMLX W. L. Jenkins (Philadelphia: Westminster Press, 1960); adapted by permission.

Book design by Gene Harris

First edition

Published by The Westminster Press ®
Philadelphia, Pennsylvania

PRINTED IN THE UNITED STATES OF AMERICA

9   8   7   6   5   4   3   2   1

Library of Congress Cataloging in Publication Data

Douglass, Jane Dempsey.
    Women, freedom, and Calvin.

    Bibliography: p.
    Includes index.
        1. Freedom (Theology)—History of doctrines—16th
century—Addresses, essays, lectures.   2. Women in
Christianity—History—16th century—Addresses, essays,
lectures.   3. Calvin, Jean, 1509–1564—Addresses, essays,
lectures.   I. Title.
    BT810.2.D68 1985   261.8'344'0924   85-8778
    ISBN 0-664-24663-X (pbk.)

Contents

Preface

This book originated as the 1983 Annie Kinkead Warfield Lectures, six lectures given at Princeton Theological Seminary March 21–24 under the title "Christian Freedom in Calvin's Theology." Dr. Benjamin B. Warfield established the lectureship in honor of his wife and directed that the lectures should deal with some doctrine of the Reformed theological tradition. The material contained in the book is essentially that of the lectures, though edited and in some places rearranged and expanded.

The nature of the lectureship, both concerned with Reformed doctrine and established to honor a woman, suggested a welcome opportunity to work out in systematic form a problem with which I had been intrigued since 1971. While preparing an article in Geneva on women in the Reformation, I had realized that Calvin's approach to the question of woman's proper role in the church was somewhat different from that of other Reformers and that I did not fully understand it. I returned to the question in 1979 when I was invited to give the Earl Cranston Memorial Lecture at the School of Theology at Claremont, this time placing the question in the context of Calvin's understanding of freedom and order.

As I continued to puzzle over Calvin's unexpected inclusion of women's silence in church among matters of order and decorum that are "indifferent," matters of human law that are adaptable to changing circumstances, it seemed that further study of this unusual aspect of Reformation thought offered a special opportunity. Here one can illustrate the usefulness of raising questions about the theological understanding of women's nature and role, and also questions about historical roles of real women, for fresh insight into classical historical theology. So often women's theological questions and women's history are marginalized as irrelevant to "serious" theology. Here they serve as an entrance point for fresh insights into Calvin's theology. Exploring this problem also provides an opportunity to see other ways in which Calvin's thought has been influenced by persons and movements contemporaneous to Calvin that are not often studied by historical theologians.

There are of course many limitations to this study; one in particular is created to a large degree by its structure as an inquiry into theological doctrine, another partly by Calvin's reticence. First, a larger-scale project would need to deal seriously with Calvin's practice with regard to freedom as well as his thought, examining his role in the consistory in disciplinary matters, for example. Such a study would in turn probably shed further light on his theology. The structuring of the study around Calvin's discussions of the doctrine of Christian freedom was a reflection of the nature of the Warfield Lectures rather than a decision that practice is irrelevant to theology. A second limitation is the frustrating difficulty in documenting actual contact between Calvin and persons and documents that one can reasonably suppose he knew. I have tried to distinguish carefully between documentable connections and assumed connections, however strongly the latter may be suggested by the circumstances.

A comment is needed about the matter of translation. Some of the writings used, such as commentaries on the Bible, exist only in Latin; some, like sermons, exist only in French. The *Institutes,* written in Latin first, was later revised by Calvin in both Latin and French editions. A modern reader will notice the masculinity of Calvin's language both about God and about people. "God" in Christian usage is a masculine noun in both Latin and French, and Calvin uses masculine pronouns to refer to God. In a discussion of historical theology there seems to be no good reason to obscure this fact by modernizing the language. In the case of language about people, Calvin's French poses the same problem as traditional English: Calvin speaks of "men" *(les hommes)* when he means "people." In the Latin texts a distinction can be made between a male person *(vir)* and a human being *(homo),* and I have often pointed out the distinction in terms used. But as the text will show, that distinction is not absolute, and *vir* will occasionally be used when one could expect *homo.* Furthermore, Calvin uses male pronouns to refer back to *homo.* Though it was tempting to try to make the translation "inclusive" in the modern sense, since existing translations of the Latin obscure the distinction completely, the resulting style proved too "feminist" for Calvin. I concluded that such an attempt would merely obscure the realities of the thought world of the sixteenth century. Therefore I have tried to clarify unobtrusively where Calvin is speaking only of male persons and where he intends to include women, occasionally substituting third-person plural for singular where the sense could better be conveyed in this way.

The structure of the book follows the systematic structure of Calvin's doctrine of Christian freedom. Chapter 1 outlines that structure in its three parts and deals briefly with the most familiar one, freedom from the bondage of law through justification by grace alone. Chapters 2 through 5 are concerned with the least-discussed part of Calvin's doctrine of Christian freedom, freedom in "indifferent things," things that are neither commanded by God nor forbidden. The example chosen as a case study is Calvin's placement of women's silence in church in the context of church order and decorum, which are "indifferent" and therefore subject to change. Chapter 2 lays the foundation for that discussion by explaining Calvin's concept of order. Chapter 3 places the discussion in the broader context of Calvin's teaching about women's public role. Chapters 4 and 5 turn to the contexts of medieval, Renaissance, and Reformation thought about women's public roles to see where Calvin reflects them and where he makes a fresh contribution. Chapter 6 then takes up the third part of Christian freedom, freedom to serve God in obedience to God's will; the focus is on service to the neighbor, the interdependence of all human beings and their mutual responsibility to aid one another.

By its nature this study will be drawn into the contemporary discussion of women's ordination, especially in Reformed churches. There are still today a few Reformed churches which feel that women's ordination is forbidden by Scripture and therefore will always be wrong. In this discussion apparently Calvin's views have always been used to oppose women's ordination and never to justify it. I am not aware of any case where his authority has been invoked in modern times to support women's ordination, though this study shows that it could have been so used. For those in churches that still struggle with the nature of the authority of the biblical injunctions to women's silence, understanding Calvin's approach to the biblical material may prove to be helpful as an example of exegesis by a respected theologian that can be used in support of women's ordination. At least it should now be more difficult to invoke Calvin's authority to forbid women's ordination.

But any attempt to use this study to make Calvin a hero in the matter of women's ordination would founder on two grounds. First, Calvin himself can be held perhaps more accountable than other Reformation theologians for Protestant women's continued subordination to men in the church, because he understood the theological possibility of giving freedom to women but decided not to make any practical attempt to do so. Second, though his position is remarkably modern for the sixteenth century, many persons today, including myself, would find Calvin's view of women's silence as an "indifferent matter" far too weak. To reflect in the life of the church the equality of all the baptized in the kingdom has become rather a theological and moral imperative. Therefore I present Calvin without apology as I believe he presented himself: open to future change on theological grounds, but far too deeply shaped by the prejudices of a patriarchal society to imagine giving up those patriarchal structures in the foreseeable future.

I would like to acknowledge with appreciation many sorts of assistance received in preparing this volume. Librarians at the School of Theology at Claremont were especially helpful in locating needed materials. The university libraries at Geneva and Strasbourg kindly opened their collections to me. Prof. Heiko A. Oberman of the University of Arizona and Prof. Bernadette Brooten of the Harvard Divinity School graciously volunteered to read the manuscript and offered helpful comments. Stephen Varvis, doctoral candidate at Claremont Graduate School, assisted with final preparation of the manuscript; and Kathryn Zimmer, student at the School of Theology at Claremont, and Anne L. Douglass, student at Wellesley College, prepared the index. Lenore Brashler typed the manuscript, educated me in the marvels of word processing, and encouraged me through that process with her interest in the material. Finally, my family was wonderfully supportive and lovingly patient throughout the project.

1

The Foundation
and Significance
of Christian Freedom

Emancipation into freedom through the liberality of God's work in the incarnation for those who have been oppressed by bondage and wearied by anxiety of conscience[1]—these are the terms in which Calvin frames his basic understanding of Christian freedom.

In the theological world of Calvin's day there are at least two distinguishable polemics in process concerning freedom. One is the debate about the natural freedom of human beings since the Fall. This is the debate about justification. What can a person since the Fall contribute to justification in God's eyes? Can someone by purely natural capacities produce genuine contrition for sin? Can a person behave in such a manner as to influence God's decision concerning salvation? Can salvation in any sense be merited? How is grace necessary for justification?

But there is a second polemic also raging regarding freedom: that is the question of freedom within the Christian community, the freedom of those who recognize themselves as members of the body of Christ. What difference has justification made in the nature of the life to be led? To what extent must Christians continue to obey the law? What kinds of church laws are proper? Should Christians feel bound in conscience to obey church laws made by mere human beings? Does the Spirit teach directly and spontaneously what Christians should do? How should Protestants observe Sunday? Or does it need to be observed at all? Must they still observe traditional seasons of fasting? Should there be candles on the altar? Or no altar at all?

Calvin felt that both questions concerning freedom had very profound pastoral implications, and he wrote prolifically on both.

In fact, they are necessarily interrelated. But it is the second to which our attention will be devoted.

From the beginning of Calvin's career as a Protestant theologian, he gave serious attention to Christian freedom. In his first edition of the *Institutes,* published in 1536, the whole sixth and final chapter, the climax of the book, is built around issues of freedom in relation to ecclesiastical power and political administration. At the opening of the chapter he calls this freedom

> a matter of prime necessity; . . . without a knowledge of it consciences dare undertake almost nothing without faltering; often hesitate and draw back; constantly waver and are afraid. . . . Unless this freedom be grasped, neither Christ nor gospel truth is rightly known.[2]

The chapter closes with Pauline advice that Calvin sees as a goad to the believer's courage: those redeemed by Christ at such great cost should not reenslave themselves to the wicked and impious desires of human beings but rather obey God.[3] Quirinus Breen says of this chapter:

> This is in many respects the most interesting. . . . One-fifth of the book is given to it. Few people have associated the name of Calvin with the idea of liberty. Let them study this great chapter.[4]

This discussion is carried through to the 1559 final edition of the *Institutes* and expanded along the way, overflowing into other sections and continuing to play a central role in Calvin's thought. A rough count in Battles's concordance[5] to the Latin text of the 1559 *Institutes* identifies over 700 uses of words derived from *libertas,* the basic Latin term for liberty or freedom.

Yet as Breen suggests, to talk about Calvin in relation to freedom—even the freedom of the Christian life—seems to many who are not unacquainted with Calvin's theology or the Reformed tradition to be an unlikely choice. After all, was it not in Geneva that Servetus was burned for heresy? Did Calvin care about Servetus's freedom? What did Calvin himself know about freedom—this rather shy man who was forced into exile by both Protestants and Catholics, who was ill so much of his life, who was threatened by Farel with the curse of God if he would not stay in Geneva in the first place against all his personal desires to devote himself to study, and who returned only reluctantly from his exile in Strasbourg? How could Calvin possibly know anything about freedom?[6] From countless examinations written by students come the simple and confident statements: "Calvin believed in predestination and denied human freedom." These are familiar objections to connecting Calvin with freedom.

Still another objection has come recently from a respected Reformation historian, Steven Ozment, that Calvin is responsible for the " 're-Catholicizing' of Protestant theology at its most sensitive point, the doctrine of justification by faith." "Calvin's teaching, like his conduct of the Genevan church, once again made good works and moral behavior the center of religious life and reintroduced religious anxiety over them."[7]

But elsewhere Ozment comments about the later period of the Reformation when Calvin was active, the second generation of the Reformation after Luther, when, Ozment feels, freedom became submerged in discipline: "Scratch a 'new papist' and one may find an old 'freedom fighter.' "[8] He goes on to argue that though the initial commitment to freedom tended to be lost in the attempt to create a discipline precisely to protect freedom, the Reformers' catechisms and church ordinances retained for a new generation of laity the earlier commitment. "The literature of discipline remained a literature of freedom. If Protestant reformers made laymen bold to resist old superstitions and tyranny, they also gave them the wherewithal to reject in time persisting and new forms of superstition and tyranny."[9]

Though I would not characterize Calvin as a "re-Catholicizer" of justification nor as a "new papist," and I hope my reasons will become clear in the following chapters, I do agree with Ozment's second point. Calvin was in a fundamental way "an old freedom fighter" who has been able to transmit Luther's commitment to Christian freedom to later generations even though Calvin himself and his secular and clerical colleagues in Geneva did not see the same implications of that freedom for practical decisions about the life-style of the church or the city which modern people would see. For example, the contemporary Reformed commitment to religious freedom has deep roots in Calvin's theology, despite the fact that Calvin's Geneva, like most of sixteenth-century Europe, placed severe restrictions on toleration of religious diversity. Therefore I will focus on Calvin's theology rather than on his practical involvement in the daily life of Geneva.[10] It is his theology of freedom that has proved enduring, giving rise to new generations of "freedom fighters" in the following centuries.

Let us return to Calvin's discussion of Christian freedom in the *Institutes*. The introduction to that discussion, quoted above, remains essentially the same through the various editions, though in 1559 Calvin adds the clarification that "freedom is especially an appendage of justification and is of no little avail in understanding its power."[11]

In all the editions Calvin outlines three parts of Christian freedom. The first is

> that the consciences of believers, in seeking assurance of their justification before God, should rise above and advance beyond the law, forgetting all law righteousness. ... We should, when justification is being discussed, embrace God's mercy alone, turn our attention from ourselves, and look only to Christ.[12]

When the conscience is concerned about standing before God's judgment, it is not the requirements of the law that count; rather, "Christ alone, who surpasses all perfection of the law, must be set forth as righteousness."[13] This aspect of freedom is related to the classic Reformation teaching of salvation by grace alone.

"The second part, dependent on the first, is that consciences observe the law, not as if constrained by the necessity of the law, but that freed from the law's yoke they willingly obey God's will."[14] Here Calvin locates the eager, ready, cheerful obedience that Christians gladly offer to God when they realize that their works are no longer measured by the standards of the law. Like children before a merciful father, they know that God will accept even their incomplete and defective works.[15]

The third part of Christian freedom has to do with outward things that are in themselves "indifferent."

> We are not bound before God by any religious obligation preventing us from sometimes using them and other times not using them, indifferently. And the knowledge of this freedom is very necessary for us, for if it is lacking, our consciences will have no repose and there will be no end to superstitions.[16]

Whereas Calvin seems to assume that the first two parts of Christian freedom will be readily understood by all his readers, since they are so basic to Protestant or "evangelical" teaching, he indicates that this third aspect dealing with "indifferent" things—that is, things that are neither commanded by God nor forbidden—introduces a "weighty controversy." On the one hand, he has in mind the tender in conscience who will begin to doubt whether linen should be used for sheets, shirts, handkerchiefs, and napkins, then go on to doubt about coarser materials, and finally wonder whether one should simply do without napkins and handkerchiefs. "For all those entangled in such doubts, wherever they turn, see offense of conscience everywhere present."[17] On the other hand,

Calvin remembers those with far less sensitive consciences who use Christian freedom as an excuse for indulging their lavish tastes in banquets, clothing, and home furnishings. Their greed and boasting defile what might otherwise be indifferent.[18]

> Surely ivory and gold and riches are good creations of God, permitted, even appointed, for human use by God's providence. And we have never been forbidden to laugh, or to be filled, or to join new possessions to old or ancestral ones, or to delight in musical harmony, or to drink wine. True indeed. But where there is plenty, to wallow in delights, to gorge oneself, to intoxicate mind and heart with present pleasures and be always panting after new ones—such are very far removed from a lawful use of God's gifts.[19]

Calvin's advice is to learn to be contented in one's own circumstances[20] and to use things thankfully for the purpose God intended.[21] But above all, "we should use our freedom if it results in the edification of our neighbor, but if it does not help our neighbor, then we should forgo it."[22] Freedom has been given to make Christians "more ready for all the duties of love."[23]

After 1543 Calvin adds a note that the Christian's freedom in spiritual things should not be understood to make obedience to government unnecessary. For as Calvin had pointed out since 1536, Christians live in both the spiritual kingdom and the political kingdom with different laws in each.[24] After 1543 the section on conscience has also been expanded considerably.[25]

What is Calvin's source for this way of describing Christian freedom? Calvin depends in substance first of all on Paul, especially in Galatians, then on Luther. In his treatise *The Freedom of a Christian*,[26] Luther sets out the basic insight that Christ has made satisfaction for all sin, leaving the Christian free from all demands of the law. The Christian then in gratitude freely and joyfully offers to serve the neighbor. There are also in Calvin's discussion some echoes of Luther's "two kingdoms," though Calvin's are not identical. In Calvin much more stress is placed on the conscience and much more on the problem of "indifferent" things than in Luther. And his phrasing of the willing obedience as obedience to the law seems to be his characteristic third use of the law—neither for pointing out sin nor for civil order and restraint of evil, but as a guide to the Christian who seeks to do the will of God. But the joyful and exuberant quality of Luther is missing, along with Luther's strong focus on the neighbor as the recipient of the Christian's willing service.

In the form, or perhaps structure, of the three parts of Christian freedom Calvin is heavily dependent on Melanchthon, the German humanist and Reformer from the Lutheran tradition. Edward Meylan has shown in detail how Calvin has adapted Melanchthon's four stages of Christian freedom from the *Loci communes* for his purposes.[27]

The use of the concept of indifferent things seems to have been nearly universal in the sixteenth-century Reformation. Humanists like Calvin, Melanchthon, and Zwingli use the Greek term *adiaphora,* while Luther apparently does not. Though both the term and the concept can be traced back through the Scholastics and the Fathers to the classical world, they never seem to have played so significant a role in Christian theology as in the sixteenth century.[28] The Augsburg Confession and the various Reformed confessions discuss the matter, as we shall see.[29] Typically the Reformers speak of ceremonies, holy days, liturgical furnishings, and choice of foods as indifferent things in which the Christian is free, but ethical issues like obedience to civil authorities on particular issues are also often included.

This dispassionate description of the sixteenth-century setting of the discussion of the "indifferent things" hardly conveys the urgency that the issue possessed for Calvin. We should listen to his introduction to a section of the *Institutes* dealing with freedom in relation to ecclesiastical law. The sections on freedom in relation to ecclesiastical power and government, originally part of chapter 6 of the 1536 *Institutes,* were later separated from the section we have just outlined and were expanded in Book IV. So we must include this material in our overview of Calvin's concept of freedom.

> It has become common usage to call all decrees concerning the worship of God put forward by people apart from his Word "human traditions." Our contention is against these, not against holy and useful church institutions which provide for the preservation of discipline or honesty or peace. But the purpose of our effort is to restrain this unlimited and barbarous empire usurped over souls by those who wish to be counted pastors of the church but are actually its most savage butchers. They say the laws they make are "spiritual," pertaining to the soul, and declare them necessary for eternal life. But thus the kingdom of Christ . . . is invaded; thus the freedom given by him to the consciences of believers is utterly oppressed and cast down. . . . Necessity ought not to be imposed upon consciences in those matters from which they have been freed by Christ; and unless freed . . . they cannot rest with God. They should acknowledge one king, their deliverer Christ, and should be governed by one law of freedom, the holy Word of the gospel, if they would retain the grace which they once

obtained in Christ. They must be held in no bondage, and bound by no bonds.[30]

In the discussions of order in the next chapter much more will be said about civil and ecclesiastical law in relation to freedom. But already one can feel the passion behind Calvin's discussion.

The only major study of the use of the *adiaphora* in the work of Calvin, that of Thomas Street, surveys the existing literature and reports that most of the scholars who compare the Reformers judge Calvin to have a more limited range of indifferent things than Luther.[31] Street himself feels that there is "not so much difference as has been claimed."[32] "[Calvin] is revealed by his doctrine of *adiaphora* as an apostle of liberty to an extent seldom recognized."[33] One unusual ethical matter Calvin includes, he notes, is the practice of usury.[34] But Street feels that Calvin presents no novel position that could claim originality.[35]

This judgment may well be valid if one studies the topics traditionally included among the *adiaphora,* such as ceremonies and, liturgical furnishings, the choice of Sunday for public worship, the covering of women's heads. However, I will try to show that Calvin takes a broader view than others of what should be considered among the *adiaphora* and does thereby make a fresh contribution to the question.

By now it has perhaps become apparent that to talk about Christian freedom in Calvin by discussing chapters of the *Institutes* devoted to it is a bit like walking into a theater during the second act of a play and leaving before the final act. The freedom discussions already sketched need to be placed into two playscripts that Calvin had in his hands. One is the biblical drama from the standpoint of eternity, the other a contemporary drama focused on that segment of the biblical drama in which Calvin himself was a participant.

The one on the grander scale, from the standpoint of eternity, is the drama of creation, sin, redemption, and re-creation. Calvin understands Adam and Eve to have been created with all the dignity of free beings; but they misused their freedom by voluntarily disobeying God and lost it.[36] So freedom belongs to the original nature of humanity. But since the fall of the first parents, human beings experience by nature only a limited and deformed freedom, the freedom to sin.[37] Though God continues to lavish gifts and common graces on fallen humanity: intellect, the knowledge of the sciences, for example, these do not create freedom.[38] But it is God's purpose to redeem and re-create what was so badly deformed.

Christ through his willing obedience to God conquered the power of evil and liberated sinners from their bondage. And with the gift of the Spirit at Pentecost, the kingdom of Christ was made manifest already in the midst of the fallen world. Those who are called by the eternal will of God and baptized into the death and resurrection of Christ, and who through the Spirit receive the gift of faith, also experience the gift of a freedom that is at least partially restored: Christians are not free from sin, but they are freed by the Spirit to obey God. This restoration or new creation of freedom in the kingdom of Christ, the Christian church, anticipates the final re-creation of all things at the end of time.[39]

So the church must be reformed according to a biblical vision of this kingdom of freedom. Calvin affirms Augustine's use of Paul's words, "Where the Spirit of the Lord is, there is freedom" (2 Cor. 3:17).[40] Calvin feels enormous urgency to help Christians of his own day see where they are in this biblical drama, to locate themselves in the kingdom where freedom reigns. He repeatedly uses the image of the exodus, the liberation of the Jews from Egyptian bondage, to describe the role of Christ, the liberator or vindicator, who frees sinners from miserable bondage in order that they may with ready obedience worship God as "the author of their freedom. . . . Our heavenly Vindicator, having liberated us by the power of his arm, leads us into the kingdom of freedom."[41]

Calvin's belief about the critical importance of the teaching of freedom is related also to the second playscript Calvin has in hand, one focused on the history of his own time in which he sees himself in relation to his immediate predecessors and contemporaries, especially the late medieval and Renaissance theologians.

On the one hand, he is clearly indebted to the late medieval vision of the freedom of God, emphasized especially in the Franciscan tradition of Duns Scotus and William of Occam. The will of God alone creates law; outside of the will of God everything is contingent. No necessity can be placed on it.[42] Listen to Calvin's reply to those who complain about the way God has changed in his dealings with humanity from the Old Testament to the New, through various times in the history of humanity. Why, some ask, could God not have been simpler and more consistent in his plan of redemption?

> This is as if they were to quarrel with God because he created the world so late . . . or because he willed to alternate winter and summer, day and night. But let us not doubt that God has done everything wisely and justly . . . even if we often do not know the reason. . . .

> Who . . . will say it is not meet that God should have in his own hand and will the free disposing of his graces, in order that he may illuminate such nations as he wills? To evoke the preaching of his Word at such places as he wills? To give progress and success to his doctrine in such way and measure as he wills? To deprive the world, because of its ungratefulness, of the knowledge of his name for such ages as he wills, and according to his mercy to restore it when he again wills?[43]

Calvin certainly echoes the late medieval stress on the freedom of the will of God here and in many other contexts.[44]

But Calvin is deeply opposed to the way the followers of William of Occam, one significant strand of late medieval theology, deal with both questions of freedom for people. They exalt natural human freedom, claiming that natural humanity since the Fall, without any special aid of grace, can love God with a perfectly unselfish love above all things. Furthermore a person must produce such love, since it is within human capacities, before God will grant grace. They are careful to place this teaching in a context of God's gracious plan of salvation which avoids blatant Pelagianism; yet many of the more Augustinian medieval theologians strongly oppose their teaching. Still, the burden of such high expectations contributed in the late Middle Ages to a religiousness pervaded by anxiety and scrupulosity.[45] It is over against that pastoral problem that Calvin, like Luther and the first generation of Reformers, insists on justification by grace alone, a doctrine that all the Reformers found more biblical than that of their predecessors. It is also in this context that one can understand why these Reformers all think the doctrine of predestination accords well with Christian freedom. If the choice of the elect is in the will of God alone, the Christian who is aware of the gift of faith within can rejoice that the Spirit is at work and feel liberated from anxiety and fear concerning eternal life.[46] As Calvin puts it:

> It makes a great difference whether you teach forgiveness of sins as deserved by just and full contrition, which the sinner can never perform; or whether you enjoin the sinner to hunger and thirst after God's mercy to show the sinner—through a recognition of misery, vacillation, weariness, and captivity—where the person should seek refreshment, rest, and freedom; finally to teach the sinner in humility to give glory to God.[47]

The second question, that of Christian freedom, seems to Calvin totally neglected by the papal church of his day. Church regulations made entirely by the clergy, such as those concerning the foods that could be eaten during periods of obligatory fasting and concerning the many days on which one must attend Mass, and the requirement of clerical celibacy for all priests, seem to Calvin very burdensome to many.

Whereas in the context of justification Calvin feels that it is grace which should be held up to the sinner, not human freedom, in the context of the Christian life Calvin believes it is precisely Christian freedom which should be announced to ease problems of doubt, anxiety, and scrupulosity. Christ's liberating work should free the Christian from a troubled conscience, from fear, from timorous obedience to laws not found in Scripture, and empower the believer by the Spirit to stand courageously against evil.

Though older scholarship often seemed to set the worlds of late Scholasticism and Renaissance humanism over against one another, recent research increasingly sees parallels and interconnections. William Bouwsma points to emphases in humanism similar to those we saw in Occamism and Scotism on the free and mysterious will of God and on the pursuit of moral perfection, but also a deepening of the sense of sin and pessimism about the human condition. He concludes:

> Renaissance humanism remained, in Luther's sense, Pelagian. The consequence was, however, that Renaissance culture in Italy, like scholastic theology in the north, helped to intensify, from both directions at once, the unbearable tension between the moral obligations and the moral capacities of the Christian that could at last find relief only in either a repudiation of Renaissance attitudes or the theology of the Reformation.[48]

Calvin chose Reformation theology rather than repudiation of a number of emphases in Renaissance thought pointed out by Bouwsma as parallels to the Reformation. One of these is the liberation of human order from the metaphysical domain so that it could be dealt with as a practical issue, on a "human scale."[49] Another is the positive focus on the human will in the context of Christian freedom, after the liberation by Christ from sin. Both Bouwsma and David Willis point out the parallels between Calvin and humanism in relation to the love of rhetoric and the role of preaching and singing in stirring the emotions and moving the will. God is seen as a rhetor who uses persuasion rather than coercion with the people of God, accommodating the Word to their capacities of understanding.[50] Such a style seems appropriate to a free people.

We see that Calvin to some extent rejects, to some extent adapts the scholastic and Renaissance theological traditions concerning freedom in his search for resources for envisioning a new style of Christian life where Christian freedom could flourish. He could also from the very beginning of his own ministry draw upon a little more than a decade of experimentation in Protestant communities like Wittenberg, Zurich, and Strasbourg. Communication among the Protestant communities was lively: books were published, visits exchanged, and letters written. Calvin also had very personal experience of the younger Protestant churches of France. And of course all Protestants retained to some degree the style of Christian living to which they had previously been accustomed. But out of all these elements and the study of the Scriptures, Calvin had to help Geneva to create a new Christian life-style to express the freedom it professed. When Calvin arrived in Geneva just after the city had declared itself for the Reformation, Calvin recalls on his deathbed,

> there was preaching and that was all. They would look out for idols, it
> is true, and burn them. But there was no reformation; everything was
> in disorder. There was, of course, the good man, Maistre Guillaume,
> and then blind Courauld. And besides them there was Maistre
> Antoine Saunier and that fine preacher Froment, who laid aside his
> apron and got up in the pulpit, then went back to his shop, where he
> chattered, and thus gave a double sermon.[51]

For Calvin a reformation requires more than preaching; it needs order. So Calvin's view of order will be the topic of the next chapter. Freedom and order belong together.

The plan for the structure of this volume is to take up each of the three aspects of Christian freedom that Calvin uses as the structure for his own discussion. In this first chapter some attention has been given to the first aspect, that of seeking assurance for justification in Christ's work rather than human work. Surely this is the most often discussed of the three, and probably the best understood.

The next four chapters will focus on the aspect of freedom related to outward things that are in themselves "indifferent." The foundation which must first be laid for that discussion is an understanding of freedom in relation to order. Then we will take one of the examples Calvin gives of "indifferent" matters, the question of women's silence in the church, and explore it in some depth.

I have chosen this example for several reasons. First, it has gone strangely unnoticed in the literature. For centuries scholars have assumed Calvin understood women's silence in church, a symbol of forbidding of public office in the church to women, to be a matter of divine law because it is taught in Scripture. I had read the *Institutes* many times myself before I noticed that Calvin had linked women's silence in church with the covering of women's heads, a regularly used example of "indifferent" things in the sixteenth century. It is perfectly logical that the two should be treated together as pieces of apostolic advice recorded in the Scriptures concerning proper decorum. But clearly there was then, and has continued to be, a different level of emotional investment in the two pieces of advice. To the best of my present knowledge, Calvin is the only sixteenth-century theologian who views women's silence in church as an "indifferent" matter, i.e., one determined by human rather than divine law. The only two articles I have found that mention this point explicitly seem to find it very hard to imagine that Calvin might have made the argument deliberately. So I have been searching for any possible evidence as to whether or not Calvin's statement was intentional.

The second reason for choosing this example is that it is one which can help people in the 1980s to understand the feelings surrounding the debate about *adiaphora* in Calvin's day. It is very difficult to find an intense theological debate today about candles on the altar or the eating of eggs and butter during Lent. But in the sixteenth-century setting these were issues about which people genuinely cared and about which serious debate took place. It took a great deal of teaching, reflection, and personal adjustment before people could regard them as "indifferent" from the standpoint of conscience. Today one still hears serious theological arguments raised in some circles against the propriety of women in public office in the church, and so one can perhaps better understand the process by which the Reformation struggled with these questions of piety.

Third, scholars regularly discuss what Calvin learned from Luther or Melanchthon, but they never ask what Calvin might have learned from any woman. This example offers that opportunity. Marie Dentière, the wife of the shopkeeper-preacher, Fromment, of whom Calvin spoke so warmly on his deathbed, published in Geneva two books that we will examine: one was the first history of the Genevan Reformation, the other a polemical document, including a "Defense for Women." We will see that the question of women's nature and proper role was under discussion.

The final chapter will take up that aspect of Christian freedom which includes willing service or obedience to God. Earlier, in comparing the *Institutes* passage explaining this aspect with Luther, I commented that there Calvin speaks much less about the neighbor who receives that service. In fact, elsewhere Calvin has much to say about the neighbor and about mutual responsibility and human solidarity. So I will focus on that aspect of Calvin's view of willing obedience, obedience to the second table of the law. Calvin's teaching on freedom is sometimes clearly intended as consolation to those who are suffering in conscience, but it always seems to be intended to strengthen the hands of those who are called to do God's work in the world. Here the strong connection between freedom and courage or boldness in Calvin's thought needs to be explored.

Christian freedom as Calvin sees it is rooted in the freedom of God. God's freedom is reflected in the freedom of the first human beings and expressed in God's will to re-create humanity through the work of Christ in the incarnation. Christ the liberator has freed fallen humanity from bondage to sin and from bondage to tyrannical human institutions that usurp God's sovereignty.

The significance of Christian freedom for Calvin is its existence within restored humanity as a sign of the presence of Christ's kingdom already alive in the midst of a fallen world. Christian freedom is the beginning of the enjoyment of a freedom that will characterize the new creation at the end of time.

2
Freedom
in God's Order

Calvin's understanding of order has to be seen from two perspectives that are at various points interrelated. The first is Calvin's sense of a cosmic order, an order in the whole universe as the result of God's decree or command, God's *ordinatio;* the second is a humanly made order or governance that is seen both in the political order and in the church, a governance that he calls *politia* in Latin, *police* in French.[1] Behind both lie God's providential care and the Spirit's lively work in nature and the human realm.

To begin with the first, the cosmic order, Calvin's reading of the biblical creation stories is certainly shaped both by the late scholastic fascination with the relation of God's ordained power to natural law and by the Renaissance preoccupation with a principle of order to be seen relating the levels of the individual, the state, and the universe. The nature of the world as created for human beings and the nature of the person as created in the image of God are both dependent on God's decree, God's *ordinatio*. But it is important to see that this order is not finalized and static: Calvin stresses the ongoing work of God in animating the universe as part of God's providential care for the creation.

> The creation of the world was completed in six days, but its administration is perpetual, and God incessantly works in maintaining and preserving its order. . . . And David teaches us that all things stand so long as the Spirit of God enlivens them, and they would immediately cease if they were deprived of his vigor.[2]

The church, too, exists by the decree, the *ordinatio*, of God. And like the universe, it is neither static nor finalized. The church begins with Adam and Eve as part of the plan of redemption. But Calvin speaks of its creation from nothing, its development, growth, and resurrection from death, as he traces its life through the covenant with Abraham, Moses, the incarnation and resurrection of Christ, and the breaking out into the Gentile world with the outpouring of the Spirit at Pentecost.[3] As a study by Benjamin Milner has described it, "The Church [for Calvin] is not so much an institution in history in which the restoration of order has been accomplished, as it is itself the history of that restoration."[4] In the church the order of the kingdom of Christ, of restored humanity, is being made manifest.[5] The growth of the church through history, like the continuation of the world itself, is possible only through the sustaining activity of the Holy Spirit. Christ as head of the church is present in its midst through the bond of the Holy Spirit when the Word is preached and the sacraments administered, as God has ordained. The gospel of Christ is known through the Word, and all things in the church should be ordered according to Christ's will.

But within the church as well as the state, created by the *ordinatio* of God, is a realm for the governing activity of God's people themselves. The ability to engage in governing activity, *politia,* is one of the marks of humanity as opposed to lower animals, one of the aspects of the image of God along with reason and reverence for God or piety.[6] In this context we can see that to call governance a human activity is not to denigrate it but to invest it with considerable dignity. Calvin is confident that people will learn to be grateful for God's magnificent ordering of the cosmos as they study the beauty and orderly movement of the heavenly bodies and days and seasons where no confusion occurs.[7] And Calvin hopes that they will learn to create orderly institutions for human life so that the evils of confusion can be avoided on earth as well. For where order fails, confusion abounds.[8] Thus governing in the church as well as in the state requires inquiry into the will of God for human life, and the use of human gifts in managing institutional life.

In view of what has been said about the importance of the concept of order in Calvin, it is somewhat surprising to find how little there is of a systematic nature in Calvin's writings about order. Calvin gives many examples of various sorts of order, but apparently he never describes order analytically.

One passage that proves to be very helpful for understanding order is in fact a discussion of providence in the treatise *Against the Libertines.* Calvin distinguishes God's governance in three ways. The first is the order of nature that applies to all creatures according to the nature given them by God in creation. God here conforms to divine laws imposed in creation. The second is the special providence that applies especially to human beings, by which God makes his creatures "of service to his goodness, justice, and judgment."[9] God intervenes in the lives of human beings to accomplish the divine will and makes use of means from the natural order. The third is God's internal governance through the indwelling Holy Spirit. Here the elect are transformed to become heirs of the new creation.[10]

One sees in this scheme that the order of nature is not to be set off alone but rather interrelated with the order of the church in which the kingdom is foreshadowed. In both orders the liveliness of the Spirit is at work. But in the church apparently God is no longer always subject to divine laws as God normally chooses to be in the order of nature, but is making a new order.

Given the difficulty in locating systematic discussions of order in Calvin himself, one can fairly ask Calvin what advice he would give a pastor or student who would ask for help in approaching such a matter. First, I think Calvin would advise the seeker to study the *Institutes,* then the commentaries. In Calvin's prefatory letter to the reader of the *Institutes,* he says:

> It has been my purpose in this labor to prepare and instruct candidates in sacred theology for the reading of the divine Word, in order that they may be able both to have easy access to it and to advance in it without stumbling. For I believe I have so embraced the sum of religion in all its parts, and have arranged it in such an order, that if anyone rightly grasps it, it will not be difficult for the person to determine both what one ought especially to seek in Scripture, and to what end one ought to relate its contents. If, after this road has, as it were, been paved, I shall publish any interpretations of Scripture, I shall always condense them, because I shall have no need to undertake long doctrinal discussions, and to digress into commonplaces.[11]

Having therefore been warned by Calvin himself that the *Institutes* and the commentaries must be read together in complementary fashion, we shall begin with the *Institutes* and then turn to the commentaries.

What can be found in the *Institutes* about the order of nature? Calvin's fundamental message is that the ordering of nature reflects God's glory, removes all excuse for ignorance of God, and communicates to the faithful God's ongoing providential care for creation. Calvin treats the order of nature here more as a source of wonder to all humanity and consolation to the believer than as a source for law or specific guidance for human behavior. For example, in Book I Calvin explains:

> The final goal of the blessed life . . . rests in the knowledge of God. Lest anyone, then, be excluded from access to happiness, God not only sowed in human minds that seed of religion of which we have spoken but revealed himself and daily discloses himself in the whole workmanship of the universe. . . . Wherever you cast your eyes, there is no spot in the universe wherein you cannot discern at least some sparks of his glory. You cannot in one glance survey this most vast and beautiful system of the universe, in its wide expanse, without being completely overwhelmed by the boundless force of its brightness. . . . This skillful ordering of the universe is for us a sort of mirror in which we can contemplate God, who is otherwise invisible.[12]

> In regard to the structure of the human body, one must have the greatest keenness in order to weigh, with Galen's skill, its articulation, symmetry, beauty, and use. But yet, as all acknowledge, the human body shows itself to be a composition so ingenious that its Artificer is rightly judged a wonder-worker. Certain philosophers, accordingly, long ago not ineptly called the human being a microcosm because a person is a rare example of God's power, goodness, and wisdom, and contains within . . . enough miracles to occupy our minds.[13]

Believers learn that there is purposefulness in the creation, with each kind endowed "with its own nature, assigned functions, appointed places and stations"; and each kind will be sustained by God till the Last Day.[14] The faithful are not to be insensitive to the "spacious and splendid house" provided with most abundant furnishings in which human beings are privileged to live, but they should gratefully meditate on God's goodness displayed in creation.[15]

One should never imagine the universe to be autonomous; rather, God's Spirit "fills, moves, and quickens all things . . . and does so according to the character that the Spirit bestowed upon each kind by the law of creation."[16] God through common grace sustains the universe and by special grace gives the gifts needed for each one's calling.[17]

Rarely in the *Institutes* does Calvin go beyond this general sense that the created order was designed to carry out God's purposes and therefore provides some direction for proper human understanding of the functions to which persons are called. One example of a somewhat more specific use of natural order for direction is in the discussion of the commandment against adultery. Here Calvin speaks of the creation of humankind to enjoy the companionship of marriage rather than to live a solitary life. He adds that to

attempt to live in celibacy if one has not received a special gift from
God would be "to contend against God and the nature ordained by
God."[18] Another example is that nature teaches obedience to
parents and other superiors as a "universal rule."[19]

It is in the commentaries and sermons on biblical passages which
focus Calvin's thought that Calvin is preoccupied with detailed
discussion and application of the law of nature or the order of
nature. Here he explains that marriage, the submission of women
to men, the authority of the preacher trumpeting God's word for
the edification of all, and the magistrate serving the common good
are reflections of the order of nature. Persons must search out the
purpose of their calling in God's plan to fulfill it properly.[20]
Creating children and the dominion of human beings over the
other creatures are other examples of the natural order created by
God.[21] Here Calvin also explains that many experiences we may
take to be natural are in fact a corruption of the natural order as
the result of original sin. Among the examples he cites are the
social inequality of persons,[22] the master-servant relationship,[23]
laziness,[24] rash divorce,[25] the annoyance of fleas and other pesky
insects,[26] and inclement air, frost, thunder, and drought.[27]

How should these disorders be dealt with? Natural disorders
over which people have no control must simply be tolerated. And
such suffering has value in proving faith and patience. But the
matter of social inequality is more complex. Though it is a sinful
deformation of the order of Genesis 1, the hierarchical social world
that Calvin accepts as inevitable in his day has some pedagogical
purpose in God's plan: the experience of "bending the neck" to
one's superiors trains sinful people to accept God's ruling despite
their arrogance.[28] So Calvin is prepared to tolerate it. Calvin thinks
polygamy is sinful, the polygamous patriarchs of the Old Testament notwithstanding. The order of nature is monogamy. But he
understands Paul to be willing to tolerate polygamy rather than
have married men abandon their wives.[29]

Still there are limits to Calvin's toleration of the disorder of
nature resulting from the Fall. Calvin tries to combat actively such
social ills as laziness and rash divorce. We will see in the final
chapter that Calvin tries to create greater social justice within the
hierarchical structure. And he clearly teaches that obedience to
parents[30] or rulers[31] or slave-masters[32] cannot be rendered if that
obedience would force disobedience to God. No superior has the
right to command what God forbids. Despite all that Calvin has
said about obedience to civil rulers as part of the order of nature,
the *Institutes* comes to a climax with the last section, which is

devoted to the obligation of civil disobedience if the ruler usurps God's sovereignty.[33] A skilled rhetorician like Calvin did not place that section in such a position by accident. Conformity to the order of nature, then, is not an absolute command; it must always take into account God's purpose for that order.

Having explored some aspects of the role of the order of nature, it is appropriate that we now turn to order in human institutions, in the church and the state. Whereas the order of nature was part of the decree of God, order in human institutions reflects to a far greater extent human freedom and governance. There is far more extended discussion of order in these contexts in the *Institutes* than we found on the subject of natural order. It appears that Calvin assumes natural order, whereas he feels the need to explain the role of human freedom in the creation of order in human institutions. We will focus on order in the church.

Already in the first edition of the *Institutes* in 1536, where Calvin was dealing with the question of proper order and government in the church, the issue was set in the context of freedom. This discussion falls in the very long sixth and final chapter entitled "Christian Freedom, Ecclesiastical Power, and Political Administration." It has been noted that the chapter begins with an explanation of the importance of the topic of Christian freedom liberating the believer from paralyzing scruples of conscience, then sets forth three principles. First, consciences of believers should rise above law-righteousness in the knowledge that no one is saved by obedience to the law; confidence is in Christ, not the law, as Galatians teaches. Second, those who are freed by Christ from slavery to the law willingly do their best to observe God's law as an expression of God's will. And third, Christians are not bound by religious obligation regarding things that are "indifferent," i.e., not intrinsically good or evil, but may use them freely, for the purpose intended by God, with thanksgiving.[34]

Calvin extensively decries the way the papal church has burdened consciences with human traditions not commanded by the Lord's Word,[35] and he wishes to liberate consciences from such superstition. But he worries that unlettered persons may be misled by this stress on Christian freedom to refuse obedience to all laws by which the order of the church is shaped. So he feels obliged to argue the positive value of church order.

> We see that some form of organization is necessary in all human society to foster the common peace and maintain concord. We further see that in human transactions there is some procedure which has to do

with public decency, and even with humanity itself. This ought especially to be observed in churches. . . . If we wish best to provide for the safety of the church, we must attend with all diligence to Paul's command that "all things be done decently and in order" [1 Cor. 14:40].[36]

Two kinds of legitimate ecclesiastical laws can be made: those useful for order, which binds the church together, and those pertaining to decorum, a fitting way things should be done in the assembly. Examples of rules concerning decorum, he says, are Paul's rules that women should not teach in church, that they should cover their heads in public, that Christians should pray publicly with knees bent and [male] heads bare, that naked corpses are not to be thrown into a ditch. Examples of rules concerning order are hours prescribed for public worship services, choice of hymns, structure of the places of worship. These are of no great importance in themselves, but it is fitting that there be stated hours and days and worship places to avoid confusion.[37]

These observances, Calvin believes, are not necessary for salvation and should not bind consciences. No piety is to be lodged in them. Christians should voluntarily obey them for the sake of peace and love but not require them "too fastidiously" of others. Churches should not despise each other because their outward discipline varies.[38]

> Is religion located in a woman's shawl, so that it is sinful for her to go out with a bare head? Is that decree of Paul's concerning silence so holy that it cannot be violated without the greatest offense? Is there in bending the knee or in covering a corpse any holy rite that cannot be neglected without guilt? Not at all. For if a woman needs such haste to help a neighbor that she cannot stop to cover her head, she commits no fault if she runs to her with head uncovered. And there is a place where it is no less proper for her to speak than elsewhere to remain silent. Also, nothing prohibits a person who cannot bend the knees because of disease from standing to pray. Finally, it is better to bury a dead man in due time than, where a shroud is lacking, to wait while the unburied corpse decays. Nevertheless, let the established custom of the region, finally, humanity itself and the rule of modesty, dictate what is to be done or avoided in these matters. In them one commits no crime if out of imprudence or forgetfulness one departs from them; but if out of contempt, this willfulness is to be disapproved.[39]

So time-bound are the church's rules concerning rites and ceremonies that even observances commanded by God himself can be changed if they become a cause of evil as circumstances change. Calvin cites the case of the brazen serpent set up by Moses:

> Thus by the testimony of the Holy Spirit Hezekiah was praised because he destroyed the brazen serpent which had been set up at the Lord's command by Moses, and which to preserve as a reminder of divine benefits was not an evil thing, if it had not begun to serve the idolatry of the people. But since the best king would have no other means of correcting impiety, he had just as good reason to break it as Moses had had to set it up.[40]

As Calvin expanded the *Institutes* over the years, this material from the 1536 edition was incorporated into a broader discussion, and sections of it were separated from one another. Women's silence in the church was moved to illustrate order rather than decorum, and the example of Hezekiah breaking the serpent was dropped. But no fundamental change was made in the point of view expressed. Calvin states a bit more sharply from 1543 on that only human constitutions "both founded on God's authority and drawn from Scripture, and, therefore, wholly divine" are approved by him.[41] In other things Christians must be left free.

> The Lord has in his sacred oracle faithfully embraced and furthermore clearly expressed both the whole sum of true righteousness, and all aspects of the worship of his majesty, and whatever was necessary to salvation; therefore, in these the Master alone is to be heard. But because he did not will in outward discipline and ceremonies to prescribe in detail what we ought to do (because he foresaw that this depended upon the state of the times, and he did not deem one form suitable for all ages), here we must take refuge in those general rules which he has given, that whatever the necessity of the church will demand to be taught for order and decorum should be tested against these. Lastly, because he has taught nothing specifically, and because these things are not necessary to salvation, and for the upbuilding of the church ought to be variously accommodated to the customs of each nation and age, it will be as fitting (as the advantage of the church will require) to change and abrogate traditional practices as to establish new ones. Indeed, I admit that we ought not to charge into innovation rashly, suddenly, nor for insufficient cause. But love will best judge what may hurt or edify; and if we let love be our guide, all will be safe.[42]

On first reading of these passages, Calvin's principal line of argument is clear: he wants to cut through what he perceives to be a mountain of religious obligations imposed on the Christian by the papal church, obligations that have created anxiety and even terror for the conscience, by sharply distinguishing Christ's commands from church laws. Only Christ's commands are binding on believers' consciences, and only Christ's clear teaching is to be seen as necessary to salvation. And Christ said very little explicitly about the structuring of church life. Ecclesiastical laws and observances fall into the category of human governing to which Christians will give assent for the sake of peace and unity while fully conscious of their provisional nature. Since the church should establish as few laws as possible and adapt them as necessary to changing conditions, such free assent to them for the sake of the community should not be burdensome.

On second reading of these passages, problems begin to arise for which the Calvin literature is hardly helpful. For it is increasingly clear in succeeding editions of the *Institutes* that one component of the human constitutions of the church under discussion is apostolic advice recorded in the Scriptures, advice that guides the church generally. Whereas Calvin is usually supposed to teach a uniform authority of all Scripture—in contrast to Luther's freer judgments about the places in Scripture where the gospel is clearest[43]—here Calvin seems to be contrasting the timeless authority of the teachings of Christ with the time-bound and provisional advice of the apostles. Yet the only criterion Calvin recognizes for admitting the apostolic advice as a general standard by which to judge church law is precisely that it is divine—because taught in Scripture—as well as human. A second component of church law, of course, is that of decisions regarding details of decorum and order which are purely human but compatible with general scriptural guidance.

To illustrate the difficulty Calvin encounters with time-bound apostolic advice, consider the problem created for Calvin by Paul's comments in 1 Corinthians 11:14, i.e., nature teaches that it is degrading for a man to wear long hair. It becomes clear that Calvin simply disagrees with Paul that this is a matter of the order of nature, and that Calvin has an exegetical method that frees him to express that disagreement.

Calvin has learned from his Renaissance humanist studies that one must always inquire into the particular historical setting in which a writing takes shape in order to understand its life setting. He is extremely conscious of the cultural changes evident over time within the Bible itself, and of the cultural difference between biblical times and his own. And so he makes use of the principle of "accommodation," that God in the incarnation and the Scriptures accommodates his message to the changing human capacity for understanding,[44] that God's Word is heard differently in different cultures. Let us see how Calvin draws upon this Renaissance insight in working with the text of 1 Corinthians.

When Calvin begins his sermons on 1 Corinthians 11, where Paul restricts the image of God to men and asserts the need for women to cover their heads while men do not, Calvin quickly points out that Paul is here dealing with traditions of propriety that have been handed down, not with doctrine. It is necessary in the church of Christ to distinguish between matters of doctrine and matters of order and government. In doctrine we are not permitted to make new laws that then must be obeyed by all. But in the realm of church government *(police)*, freedom is left to human decision. Churches can differ in form and exterior order. Paul commends the Corinthian church for having respected its traditions, for it is not wise to be constantly changing for frivolous reasons.[45]

Paul is well aware, Calvin thinks, that religion and sanctity do not consist in matters of covering the head or not.[46] But since Paul sets up as perhaps a hypothetical example—as Calvin suggests—the image of a woman preaching or leading a congregation in prayer with her head uncovered, Calvin agrees that everyone would be horrified and would find such a spectacle lacking in decorum.[47]

> It is not necessary for us to have written law from God, or many testimonies. Nature suffices to give us this inclination not to be able to see what is contrary to decency, but all will turn away their eyes from it.[48]

Paul teaches the veiling of women as a sign of their proper subordination according to the order of nature, lest that order be changed and perverted.[49]

If Calvin here indicates that nature dictates proper order, elsewhere in the sermon he acknowledges that nature's teaching is less clear. He realizes that in some cultures women display their hair and men cover theirs; an example is the wearing of turbans in the East by men. Though he seems to suggest that people should not measure God by their own customs in the light of varying cultures, he goes on to indicate that men's wearing of miters and turbans makes them seem to have become women, and this disorder, this changing of the order of nature, is an indication of the world's perversity.[50] Still, in his commentary on 1 Corinthians 11 he finds no sin in a male preacher wearing a skullcap in the pulpit to keep his head warm; he can nod to propriety by doffing his cap in the sight of the congregation, then replacing it on his head.[51]

In a sermon dealing with the same context, Calvin shows his

awareness of Paul's setting in a particular moment in history when he comments on Paul's contempt for men with long hair as against nature (1 Cor. 11:14). With great respectfulness, Calvin explains that Paul speaks here only of the custom prevalent in Paul's day in the countries where he spoke. For in Geneva, France, and Germany, as in antiquity among the Jews, men were accustomed to wearing long hair and beards. The point, then, Calvin thinks, is that one should inquire whether customs are good, decent, according to the law of nature, edifying, of good example. If so, one should not be eager to change and bring about confusion. But if the customs are not appropriate to God's word, then there should be change.[52]

Calvin discusses at length the point that Christ is the head of the whole church, of men and women whom he has freed from their sins. Paul's whole distinction here between men and women, and his teaching about how they should behave, has to do with the maintaining of order *(police)*,[53] not therefore with doctrine.

In both his commentary and his sermons on 1 Corinthians 11, Calvin raises the apparent conflict of this text with Galatians 3:28: "There is neither . . . male nor female . . . in Christ Jesus." In Galatians, he says, Paul is speaking about the spiritual kingdom of Christ, where indeed there is no difference between male and female, between master and servant, rich and poor, between a king and a shepherd or a mechanic, a Frenchman and a German, a pastor and a lay person. Calvin emphatically and repeatedly argues that the gift of the image of God in creation and the restoration of it in the kingdom apply equally to men and women, along with the gift of the Holy Spirit and participation in worship and the sacrament.[54] Women can take comfort in the fact that when the kingdom comes, all differences in rank will disappear. But until this world passes away, the order of creation by which man was created first and woman from man, and thus subservient to man, remains the pattern according to which governing in external things *(police)* is organized.[55] But God has not given men an infinite empire, to hold women under their feet or oppress them or tyrannize over them.[56] Great inequalities in the social sphere, between men and women, between rich and poor, are legacies of the Fall and the deformation of God's creation by sin; and they are a sign of God's wrath and punishment for sin.[57]

Calvin then draws out as the significance of the passage for our instruction that all human beings are made for each other, to be useful and helpful to each other, that there should be mutual communication for the common good, and reciprocal duty. The graces which each has received are for the service of others, and each should conform to the other in all humanity.[58] This concept of "double" or "mutual" subjection of men and women seems unusually marked in Calvin and can be found elsewhere in his commentaries as well.[59] Even when Calvin is most insistent that male superiority is so much an aspect of nature that it applies throughout society, not merely in particular relationships like marriage, he immediately turns this point to show that men's contributions to society are for the benefit of women.

> It is indeed true that men today are like canals by which God makes his grace to flow down onto women. For from where do industry and all the arts and sciences come? From where does labor come? From where do all the most excellent things come, those that we prize the most? It is certain that all this comes from the side of men. God then wills that men serve the usefulness of women, as experience demonstrates.[60]

Calvin seems as much concerned to protect the authority of the magistrates in this life against the radicals who want to destroy that authority as to protect the superiority of men over women. He argues that Christ did not intend to abolish order among us and bring everything into confusion. Without order human life would be like that of the beasts.[61] By the goodness of God we are spared from the total impact of the Fall: the sun and moon are in the skies, the earth produces fruit, Christ gives us celestial felicity and eternal salvation and in this world nourishment, order, and government so that everything is not confused and corrupted. We should remember this and magnify the goodness of God.[62]

Calvin reminds women that they should keep perspective on their situation and willingly, without anger or discontent, bear the yoke which God has placed upon them. For it is a small thing and transitory that in this world men have some slight superiority, for the whole thing is only a figure, as Paul says, and one day those in authority will be put down.

> And if he [Paul] says that women are not at all marked with the image of God like men, in regard to this temporal state which passes and vanishes with the figure of this world . . . they see that God has created us all in his image, both males and females, and that however much this image has been abolished by the sin of Adam, it is renewed by our Lord Jesus Christ; that when we are regenerated by the Holy Spirit, it is as if God declares that he dwells in us, that we are his temples.[63]

So the church stands both in this transitory world and in the coming eternal kingdom. Its order reflects the social inequities of the fallen world, but its source of life is the Spirit who is already creating within it the kingdom of God where these inequities will disappear. In Christ's kingdom all human hierarchy will vanish.

We have seen that Calvin's view of social order is not a static, fixed, rigid system, but one which is rooted in God's decree, an expression of the will of God, which may be expressed in varying forms in different ages and cultures. It reflects an awareness of and respect for natural law, or the order of nature, or the order of creation, but at times even this natural order seems less than absolute. We have seen that Calvin finds Paul's view of long hair for men as contrary to the order of nature merely a cultural issue, not a religious one. Calvin includes Paul's injunction to women's silence in church, understood for centuries to be related to the order of creation, among the details of church order or decorum subject to change as culture changes. Still another sort of example might be Calvin's treatment of the Sabbath. In his commentary on Genesis he appears to consider the hallowing of the seventh day as a day of rest a divine law for human life built into the order of creation.[64] Yet in other contexts we find him arguing strongly that the choice of a day for rest and worship lies within the realm of Christian freedom. Christians are not obliged to choose either the seventh or the first day of the week, though the arguments for choice of the first day for worship are very strong. The choice of a solemn day is a matter of maintaining discipline and good order. Calvin could have found this view of Sabbath in Augustine, Bucer, and the Augsburg Confession.[65]

Where should we look for the source of such a view of order? What is the context in which we should read Calvin's explanations? Passerin d'Entrèves in his discussion of the history of legal philosophy has pointed out that two different changes took place in the world in which Calvin's thought took shape. First, the idea of sovereignty comes into a new focus in the sixteenth century; Bodin deserves much credit for it. "All law must go back to an ultimate power which expresses and sanctions it. The holder of that power is the source of the law. He is therefore above the law."[66] The concern for sovereignty, for positive law, goes back to the recovery of Roman law in the eleventh century and proved very controversial in the generations that followed. One consequence of this idea appeared to be the undermining of the possibility of natural law, though in fact ways were found to permit the two understandings of law to coexist.

The second development, which also seemed to be a threat to the idea of natural law, was the late medieval voluntarism of Scotus and Occam, their focus on the freedom of God's will. D'Entrèves sees this development as the extension of the idea of sovereignty to the arena of moral law. The definition of the good is to be found in the fact that God wills it. "Natural law ceases to be the bridge between God and man. It affords no indication of the existence of an eternal and immutable order."[67]

D'Entrèves finds it very understandable, therefore, that Luther and Calvin and their followers in the sixteenth century should downplay the tradition of natural law because of their rooting in late medieval voluntarism, without ever completely abandoning natural law, while stressing the positive law of the state as "ultimately grounded upon the will of God."[68] He sees another shift at the end of the century, when there was a revival in Protestantism of the idea of natural law.

Though some details of d'Entrèves's discussion would be corrected by recent scholarship, he helps us put into perspective the tension in Calvin between natural order and the freedom of God's Spirit. And though he gives no evidence at all from the Reformers themselves, we have already discussed the fact that Calvin is often viewed as strongly shaped by the late medieval voluntarist tradition, especially by Scotus.[69] Surely we should see the late medieval uneasiness about earlier views of natural law as the context for Calvin's choice not to build a stronger and more consistent case for the authority of the order of nature for human conduct.

One striking example in Calvin of the voluntarism common to the late medieval Franciscans is his discussion of Deuteronomy 8:1–4: a person does not live by bread alone but by everything that proceeds out of the mouth of the Lord. Calvin denies that this passage has to do with the life of the soul only. He points out that though we are accustomed to being nourished by bread and wine, and we observe that a person weak with hunger is revived by eating familiar foods, Moses is telling us that the bread and wine have no power in themselves. They are dead creatures that cannot impart life.

> It is true that the bread will indeed be a means of refreshing a person, and God wishes to make use of it. But is it necessary for us to attach our lives to bread and wine? Not at all. But it is necessary to see that God has constituted this order in nature, but it is not to detract from his praise nor to despoil him of his right. But rather if he wishes to deploy his power by means of his creatures, it is to show

that he has them all in his hand, and that he is able to dispose of
them according to his good will.[70]

Unlike a human father who has only bread with which to nourish
his children, God could use other means. God's power is not shut
up in the things he has made. He nourished the Jews in the
wilderness with manna, and he could use other means.[71]

Here we see the Franciscan spirit, which insists that what appear
to be laws of nature, cause and effect, are in fact merely the order
God has chosen; God could have created a quite different order.
Though in fact God normally governs the world according to these
chosen means so that the order of nature appears to us to be
reliable, God can choose to break through this order in miraculous
fashion.[72]

Calvin in preaching on John the Baptist's claim that God can
raise up children of Abraham even from stones (Luke 3:8) extends
this view of the contingency of the material order to that of the
spiritual order of the church. Calvin grants that the "papists" are
right in claiming that Jesus has promised never to abandon his
church. But they are wrong in presuming that God needs them to
be the church, in saying:

> We are descended since the apostles by a continual succession . . . so
> that it is necessary that God declare himself here, and that he live in
> the midst of us; and if he would disavow us, God would be change-
> able. When then the Papists wish to enclose the church in their den of
> thieves . . . they abuse themselves. . . . St. John says that God will work
> so that he will conserve his Church, not at all at the appetite of hu-
> man beings and according to their imaginations but by his high and
> incomprehensible power.[73]

"God in maintaining his church is not subject to any natural order,
but he works there in a strange fashion."[74] In a miraculous way out
of natural confusion God creates the church as though he made
human beings out of stones, and even more than human beings—
companions of the angels, inheritors of the kingdom of heaven.[75]
Calvin clearly affirms that the promises of God are reliable, that
God will maintain his church in the world; but it is presumptuous
to imagine that God is bound by a particular order for the church.

> In discussing infant baptism Calvin even points out that . . . when the
> apostle makes hearing the beginning of faith he is describing only the
> ordinary arrangement and dispensation of the Lord which he com-
> monly uses in calling his people—not, indeed, prescribing for him an
> unvarying rule so that he may use no other way.[76]

Still another source for Calvin of this dynamic view of order would have been sixteenth-century Renaissance thought. Recent studies like that of Bouwsma stress that there coexists in the Renaissance with Stoicism, marked by its negative view of social change,[77] an Augustinian strain of thought. "The historicism of the Renaissance . . . was distinctly not a function of the Stoic tendencies in humanism, which could only view mutability with alarm, but rather of the Augustinian tradition, in which God's purposes were understood to work themselves out in time."[78] Bouwsma sees Calvin as an illustration of the Augustinian strain in humanism, one who took account of historical change and practical circumstances in his study of church history and of the Bible. "For Calvin fallen man seems to confront God in history rather than in nature."[79] According to Lucien Richard, "For Calvin the fulfillment of the Kingdom included within it the renovation of the world, the restoration of the created order. At the very core of Calvin's eschatology was the belief that the coming of God's kingdom transforms the created world."[80]

It should not be difficult now to see how Calvin's thought about freedom and order in the church provides an important part of the systematic basis for his many ecumenical exhortations which McNeill and Nijenhuis have so ably drawn together.[81] In his commentary on the opening verses of 1 Corinthians 11, Calvin praises Paul's modesty in avoiding the pitfall of worldly teachers who expect "their own example to be looked upon as completely binding." Paul, rather, "points himself and others back to Christ as the one exemplar of right action." The unwritten traditions that Paul speaks here of handing down, Calvin thinks, do not have to do with doctrine or things necessary to salvation but with matters of order and polity. "We know that each church is free to set up the form of polity that suits its circumstances, and is to its advantage, because the Lord has not given any specific directions about this."[82] But Paul gives sound advice to help the Corinthian church do all things decently and in order.

Do statements such as these mean that the form by which the church is governed does not matter? Hardly. Calvin sees in the example of the New Testament as he reads it a pattern of government of the church by a fourfold ministry: that of bishops or ministers, elders, deacons, and teachers, chosen by the community on the basis of graces they have received. This fundamental pattern seems to him to be eminently suited to the church as the people of God, as the body of Christ, as a holy priesthood.[83] It is a pattern that shares leadership among those of different gifts and makes all in authority subject to the discipline of others. But Calvin also understands the practical reasons that produced in time the monarchical episcopate in the early church,[84] and he is quite approving of the existence of the office of bishop in some churches of his own day, where its function is properly understood.[85]

To use an expression which John Leith has applied to the Reformed tradition more broadly: for Calvin polity is important, but it is also radically subordinate to the gospel.[86] This is the fundamental reason why Calvin is constantly urging that churches that differ in polity or ceremony or in doctrines other than those most fundamental to the Lordship of Christ must not treat each other with contempt or lack of charity.[87] The preaching of the gospel calls the church into being. The preaching and hearing of the gospel, and the administration and reception of the sacraments, shape the life of the church by God's command. But governance in external matters will permit a variety of forms adapted to changing circumstances. Not any form will do, but those forms which permit the communication of the gospel and the expression of the life of a community of love and mutual responsibility. Above all, the order of the church must reflect the freedom of the Holy Spirit to give to each member of the church differing gifts that are needed in turn by the community at large.

> It is expedient for the common salvation of the body that no individual should be so furnished with the fulness of gifts as to despise his brothers with impunity. . . . The soundness of the church is preserved by this most beautiful order and symmetry, when every individual . . . imparts to the common good what he has received from the Lord without preventing others from doing so. To invert this order is to fight with God, by whose ordination it was appointed.[88]

Order, then, is for Calvin a good gift of God that comes to humanity in different ways. Natural order forms the context in which human life is led and provides some guidance for the good life, but it is by no means absolute in determining moral behavior. In fact Calvin realizes that some behavior that the Bible attributes to the order of nature is culturally determined. Political order and ecclesiastical order derive from God's gift to humanity of the power to govern, and they represent realms where humanity is free to adapt and transform tradition as necessary to carry out God's purposes in a changing world. Both kinds of order are informed by the ongoing lively activity of the Holy Spirit, who is moving human order in the direction of the freedom of the kingdom of God.

Such a dynamic view of order rooted in a vision of freedom surely underlies the energetic espousal by the later Reformed tradition of the slogan *Ecclesia reformata semper reformanda est:* The reformed church is always to be reformed.

3
Women's Freedom in Church Order: Calvin's View

Among his examples of matters in which the church is free to change its mode of life, Calvin includes the admonition of Paul for women to keep silence in the church. This is startling in view of the widespread assumption in the older literature that Calvin accepts Paul's teaching of the subjection of women wholeheartedly and holds women in low esteem. Some put it more colorfully, as, for example, in this quotation from an early twentieth-century historian of women's place in Western society: "Many reformers, especially Calvin and the Scotch ministers, have raved so vehemently against the 'lust of the flesh' that they left no doubt in regard to the hostile attitude of Christianity toward women."[1] A little more recently, in 1931, Georgia Harkness concluded from her study of Calvin's ethics, "It is by no accident that the Presbyterian church has refused to ordain women, or to open to them anything like equality with men in religious offices. Calvin would have none of it."[2]

Though assertions of this sort are commonplace, in fact there has been very little scholarly study of Calvin's attitude toward women and even less study of Calvin's view of women's freedom in the church. Most of the literature deals with marriage, manners, and morals. Therefore it seems appropriate to select this issue as a case study to see whether we have properly understood Calvin's view of order. It surely will be one of the most difficult test cases available. We will first look at the few recent studies that exist, then explore what Calvin has had to say on the subject. The following two chapters will attempt to reconstruct the sixteenth-century context in which to evaluate his position as it now appears from the sources.

The only monograph on the subject of Calvin's view of the relation of men and women is that of André Biéler in 1963, *Man and Woman in Calvin's Ethic.* This is a learned and wide-ranging study of Calvin's thought on love, marriage, celibacy, divorce, adultery, and prostitution in the sixteenth-century context which gives a far more balanced picture of these matters than was formerly available. But only a brief five-page section focuses on the place of woman in church and society, the more public arena with which the present study is particularly concerned. Biéler describes Calvin's understanding of the relation between men and women as one of differentiated equality: a fundamental equality with differentiated function. Without any reference to the *Institutes* in this section, Biéler quotes a few passages from the commentaries while suggesting that order in the church and, even more, order in the society at large are "always, let us remember, a very relative and very approximate expression of the primitive order of creation" due to sin, and they vary according to circumstances, times, and places.[3] In the book's conclusion he comments that though there is no doubt that Calvin expected women to be subordinate in his own society,

> it is very important to underline that, in the thought of Calvin, social inequality of the spouses is a fact tied to history, a fact of political nature, contingent, while their spiritual equality is an essential and unchangeable quality. One finds again here this capital distinction in reformed doctrine between that which is spiritual and fundamental on the one hand and that which, on the other hand, is "political," that is to say, fluctuating and modifiable at the will of circumstances, adaptable to historical evolution.[4]

Biéler's perception fits very well the view of order that we developed in the last chapter. But his brief comments lack the documentation to be persuasive to those disinclined to believe him. And there certainly are those who see the matter very differently.

Two apparently independent articles concerning Calvin's view of the role of women were published in 1976. One, by John Bratt, describes Calvin as holding a view of "qualified but definite subordination of woman" to man, based on his study of passages from Calvin's commentaries on Genesis 2, the letters of Paul to Corinth, Ephesus, and Timothy, and a few of Calvin's own letters.[5] He acknowledges that Calvin believes women should be treated with respect and dignity, that they receive spiritual gifts from God and have the hope of salvation, and even that women might be permitted to rule nations if they inherit the throne, and to have equality in conjugal rights and the initiation of divorce. But they are excluded from all public office in the church because they are subordinate to men. Bratt concludes, "This hierarchical arrangement in Calvin's estimation is to be permanently binding. It permits of no alteration, modification, or cancellation. 'God hath set an order,' says he, 'which may in no wise be broken, and must continue even to the worldes end.' "[6] But then Bratt adds an appendix with what he calls "A Few Collateral Considerations," pointing out certain indications of hesitation and flexibility on Calvin's part, drawing almost exclusively on the *Institutes,* including a few of the passages discussed in the previous chapter.[7]

The second 1976 article, by Willis DeBoer, follows a pattern similar to Bratt's. It opens with a firm judgment that "Calvin's views on women were very traditional. To some modern ears they sound outrageous, even despicable. Calvin knew where he stood on the matter and he stood his ground. In writing his commentaries and preaching his sermons, he was rigorously consistent: women are subject to men by virtue of their created place in this world and by virtue of the curse of sin that is on them. Women may neither rule nor teach men."[8] Calvin forbade women to hold any public office in the church, including that of deacon.[9] DeBoer moves into the commentaries, noting that Calvin reads Genesis through the eyes of Paul, finding justification in the whole of Scripture for Paul's view that women were created subject to men. DeBoer then adds a section entitled, "Some Open Doors for Modification," noting some passages that seem to suggest the possibility for change. Yet he is troubled by the concessions Calvin seems to be making and their effect on Calvin's own principles. He is aware that Calvin has sometimes "adjusted" the obvious sense of Scripture to accommodate his presuppositions about the order of nature, but that he has also sometimes been open enough to realize there are unsolved problems.[10]

A third article dealing with Calvin's view of women's authority, published even more recently by Rita Mancha, cites many of the same passages in Calvin, though omitting those from the *Institutes* section on Christian freedom, and agrees that Calvin is very consistent in teaching women's subordination in all aspects of life. She finds too few examples of qualification of that view to be troubled by them.[11]

As interpreters of Calvin, can we do no better than to assert

Calvin's "rigorous consistency" and then perhaps point out the contradictions and qualifications? Is there no more satisfying way to make sense out of the numerous passages where Calvin discusses women's role in society? What can be meant by "rigorous consistency" where there are admittedly numerous concessions?

It seems to me that these attempts to describe Calvin's view of women's role in society and in the church quite correctly assume that Calvin remains under the influence of a culture that presupposes the superiority of men over women in social relations. In fact, by taking so little account of this cultural context, they probably underestimate rather than overestimate that influence. Nearly the whole Christian tradition that Calvin knew had read the Bible in this light. Furthermore, Calvin's convictions about the unity of the Scriptures make it a virtue to find the harmony behind apparently discordant passages of the Bible. This makes it all the more unlikely that we have understood Calvin if we describe him as Bratt and DeBoer have done.

However, I believe that Bratt and DeBoer are correct in perceiving that Calvin has to struggle to find a consistent way to understand the biblical texts dealing with women. The time-honored theological answer of the tradition Calvin knew, the divine subordination of women, did not fit either the totality of the biblical texts he studied or the sociological realities of the sixteenth-century world around him. Whereas Calvin repeatedly finds "easy" solutions that "clearly" dispose of difficult problems like discrepancies among the Gospel accounts,[12] he at times writes pages trying to answer the questions posed to him by biblical texts concerning women.

None of the three interpreters cited has attempted to place Calvin's thought about the role of women in the broader systematic context of Calvin's concept of order. Mancha has assumed that order is synonymous with the order of nature and is static, though Bratt and DeBoer realize that Calvin sometimes disagrees with Paul about the order of nature.[13] The dynamic sense of order in Calvin, which we set forth in the last chapter, would certainly suggest that this context is the key to finding some coherence in Calvin's position. And neither Bratt, DeBoer, nor Mancha has attempted to follow Calvin's own advice to use the *Institutes* as the systematic context within which to read the commentaries. Therefore I shall try to use this approach to the material.

What then does Calvin say in the *Institutes* about the role of women in church and society? If one begins with the 1536 edition, one could easily conclude that at that time he was not greatly interested in the question of women's place. When he discusses human creation, he describes Adam as the "parent of us all," made in the image and likeness of God; and it was Adam who slipped into sin.[14] Eve is simply absent from the context, for good or for ill; "Adam" seems to represent humankind. In the section dealing with the Ten Commandments, we find no mention of any subordination of women; "parents" are to be honored, and husbands and wives are to regard themselves as married in the Lord.[15] We are not to separate husband from wife or wife from husband by covetousness. And even in a summary of the duties of obedience of the people to rulers and children to parents, no mention is made of wives' subjection to their husbands.[16] Nor can this subjection be found in his discussion on the non-sacrament of marriage.[17]

Perhaps another dozen references to women can be noted, all anonymous except for Priscilla, Eve, and the Virgin Mary.[18] There are two somewhat disparaging references, one to the credulity of "mere women"[19] and the other to "old-womanish little ceremonies,"[20] the second of which would disappear from the *Institutes* after 1539.

And then there is the passage, quoted in the last chapter, from the discussion on Christian freedom about decorum and order, including the silence of women in church. Calvin provides the following summary of the matter:

> Establishing here no perpetual law for ourselves, we should refer the entire use and purpose of observances to the upbuilding of the church. If the church requires it, we may not only without any offense allow something to be changed but permit any observances previously in use among us to be abandoned.[21]

The casual way in which Calvin links Paul's advice for women to cover their heads and to be silent in church with practical matters like whether arthritics need to kneel and how to bury corpses, matters that no one has ever claimed to be dictated by Scripture, is startling. He certainly makes clear that no eternal law of God requires women's silence in church, and that customs which serve the edification of the church in one era can well be changed in another if they cease to serve the edification of the church.

One can conclude on the basis of the 1536 edition of the *Institutes* that the young humanist scholar Calvin, emerging from his studies into a more public role, shows no interest in making the traditional points about the subjection of women in marriage and the family. It is not clear whether the omission is deliberate or unintentional. And the only point he makes about women's public role in the church falls in the chapter on Christian freedom: Paul's rule that women should be silent is historically conditioned and belongs in the realm of church traditions that should not be made binding on Christian consciences. Nowhere is there any indication of conscious polemic concerning women's role.

Turning to the 1559 final and much-expanded edition of the *Institutes,* one notices some changes. Calvin does seem more aware generally of the place of women in biblical history. Yet Eve is very nearly missing still from discussions of creation, the image of God, and the Fall. Both the uprightness of the first human being and the Fall are related to Adam, apparently understood as humankind.[22] A vague reference to the unfaithfulness of the woman in relation to sin can be found,[23] but clearly Calvin still passes by the traditional opportunity to castigate Eve for tempting Adam to sin.

In a discussion of the renewal of the image of God through Christ, newly added in the 1559 edition, Calvin inserts abruptly in a polemical manner this point: "But the statement, however, in which only the man is called by Paul the image and glory of God and woman is excluded from this degree of honor is clearly to be restricted, as the context shows, to the political order."[24] "Political" here is to be understood as the realm of human governance, which Calvin discusses in the last chapter. Inferiorities in women's status again seem to be considered by Calvin to be a matter of human, historical judgments, and he feels the need to correct the apparent meaning of Paul's statement lest his readers understand from it that women lack the created image of God.

By now Mary Magdalene,[25] Hagar, Sarah, Rachel, and Rebecca,[26] as well as Mary[27] the mother of Christ, have moved onto the stage of biblical history related by Calvin. So have the widows of the early church whom Calvin believes to have exercised a public ministry as deacons.[28] Since 1543 he has explained that there were two sorts of deacons in the early church, those who administered funds for the poor, and those who actually cared for the poor. He believes that women were only permitted to undertake this latter public office, and that the widows discussed in 1 Timothy 5 as taking a vow were deacons. But there is some suggestion that he realizes not everyone will agree with him as he proceeds: "If we accept this (as it is certainly to be accepted), there will be two sorts of deacons."[29] In earlier editions he had phrased it a bit differently: "If we accept this exposition, as it is worthy of acceptance, seeing that it is founded in good reason . . . ."[30] One hears in these parenthetical comments some defensiveness in his insistence that women did indeed hold public office in the early church.[31]

Calvin fears that his readers may accuse him of inconsistency with his repudiation of monastic vows, since he holds that the women deacons of the early church took a vow of celibacy. So he explains that the deacons did not regard this vow of celibacy as religious in itself but rather as a necessary condition to carry out the public ministry to which they had pledged themselves. "Unless they were independent and free of the marital yoke, they were not able to carry on that function."[32] So the vow of celibacy of the women deacons was purely functional in relation to their task, and it was not so binding that it could not be revoked if they were unable to maintain celibacy. However, Paul's conditions that the widows be over sixty years of age and have already proved their contentment with a single marriage make it unlikely that they will be unable to remain celibate.[33] So Calvin sharply distinguishes the early church widows, living under a vow of celibacy in order to free themselves to perform a public ministry in the church, serving the poor, from the medieval nuns, whom he describes as having been received into a cloistered life of idleness in their youth.[34]

There is no explanation in Calvin's discussion as to why male deacons can be married but female ones cannot. Possibly he presumes simply the practical advantage of keeping the woman free from the responsibility of managing a household; or perhaps he has in mind the church's obligation to support the widow-deacons. But possibly he also acknowledges at least a relative freedom of a single woman from subordination to men. Elsewhere, however, he makes clear that women's subordination in society is not restricted to marriage.[35]

Though women had certainly once been deacons, Calvin thinks women should not in his day baptize infants. Calvin takes up this question polemically in 1543 in the context of the issue of "emergency baptism"; he is greatly concerned about the midwives' practice of baptizing newborn infants who seem unlikely to live long enough to be presented to the priest for baptism. Calvin uses two basic arguments. First, there is no "emergency," no "danger" to justify a private baptism, because children of the covenant will not be barred from the kingdom of heaven just because they were not immersed in water. Second, Christ linked the preaching of the word and the administration of the sacraments in the same public office, and no one should usurp an office to which that person has not been duly called. Calvin explicitly indicates that neither men nor women should baptize unless called to the office of pastor, and he believes that women were called to that office only among heretics in the early church. So his discussion of evidence concerning women baptizing in the early church and prohibitions of it from certain of the Fathers should be read not as a debate about whether women should exercise public ministry but rather as a debate about "emergency baptism." Calvin freely concedes the fact that lay men and women had baptized in "emergencies" since antiquity. But he appears unaware of the role of women deacons in regular baptisms in the ancient church.[36]

When Calvin discusses infant baptism and the objections to it rooted in the lack of explicit biblical evidence for it, he alludes in a different way to women's place in the early church. He takes the position that if the argument from silence should be used to forbid infant baptism, women would not be permitted to participate in the Lord's Supper either. But he concludes, "Here we are content with the rule of faith. For when we weigh what the institution of the Supper implies, it is also easy to judge from this to whom the use of it ought to be granted."[37]

Another new polemical section added in 1559 falls into the context of the discussion of the true humanity of Christ. Calvin attacks the "new Marcionites" who

> to disguise their error—to prove that Christ took his body out of nothing . . . too haughtily contend that women are "without seed." Thus they overturn the principles of nature. But this is not a theological issue. . . . Accordingly I shall not touch on matters that belong to philosophy and medicine.[38]

But he goes on to deal with the biblical matter that Christ's genealogy is apparently recounted only according to Joseph's lineage, arguing in response that Mary came from the same family. If Scripture names only males, "Must we then say that women are nothing? Why, even children know that women are included under the term 'men' [*viris*]."[39] Though in the "political order" a preferential position is given to the male sex in carrying the family name through the male line, it is also true that according to law in slavery "the offspring follows the womb." Thus the law, as well as the common custom to call mothers "engenderers," supports the understanding that Christ's humanity was truly derived from his mother's body.[40] One sees Calvin here scornful of theologians who undercut Mary's role on the basis of bad biology or bad biblical exegesis.

What of Calvin's final treatments of marriage in the *Institutes*? No mention of the subjection of women to men appears in the treatment of the commandment to honor parents, though Calvin understands the Fifth Commandment to include honoring all those whom God has placed over us, including parents, church ministers, and secular rulers.[41] Nor does it appear in the discussion of the commandment against adultery,[42] or in the section discussing the marriages of the New Testament ministers. According to Paul, the apostles "not only kept their wives but took them about with them."[43]

The only explicit teaching of women's subjection I have found is in the context of the submission of the church to the Word of God. What had been in the 1536 edition a brief allusion[44] has since 1543 been developed more fully metaphorically to picture the church which "allows itself to be taught by the Holy Spirit through God's Word."

> And what wonder if Christ's bride and pupil be subject to her bride-groom and Teacher, so that she pays constant and careful attention to his words! For this is the arrangement of a well-governed house, that the wife obey the husband's authority. This is the rule of a well-ordered school, that there the teaching of the schoolmaster alone be heard. For this reason, the church should not be wise of itself, should not devise anything of itself but should set the limit of its own wisdom where Christ has made an end of speaking.[45]

But then only two chapters later comes again the discussion of church order and decorum previously quoted from the 1536 edition. The context is still that of Christian freedom: how to provide organization for the church to foster peace and concord without binding consciences to order and decorum, which are both subject to human culture and changing circumstances. This time the covering of women's heads is still given as an example of decorum, but women's silence in the churches has been reclassified as a matter of order. Yet, as before, both sorts of ecclesiastical constitutions should be honored for the good functioning of the community but held with a free conscience. And both can be changed as circumstances require for the upbuilding of the church.[46]

Finally, Calvin makes no effort to exclude women from this general admonition to the church: "It is clear that every member of the church is charged with the responsibility for public edification according to the measure of that member's grace, provided it be done decently and in order."[47]

Our survey of the 1559 *Institutes* suggests that after many years of preaching, teaching, and administering the church, after publishing all his New Testament commentaries and about half the Old Testament commentaries, Calvin's selection of what is important to grasp theologically in order to understand the Scriptures properly still virtually excludes positive teaching of the subordination of women. He restates with no fundamental change his original conviction that Paul's admonition for women to be silent in church and to cover their heads is historically conditioned advice, not perpetual divine law that should bind the conscience. In almost every case where he refers to the *fact* of women's subordinate role in society, he clarifies that this is a matter of the "political" order of human governance. Finally, three of the four new polemical sections dealing with women—those dealing with the image of God in women, Christ's descent through Mary, and public ministry of the deacons in the early church—have the effect in the sixteenth century of strengthening the dignity of women's position.

Let us turn now to the biblical commentaries of Calvin on key passages dealing with women's place in church and society, following roughly the order in which Calvin worked through the Bible in sermons and published commentaries. But the value of this method for tracing development should not be exaggerated. The critical apparatus of the *Corpus Reformatorum* edition is inadequate for such study. Though the commentaries on the New Testament epistles were published over about a twelve-year period beginning in 1539, they were according to Parker "thoroughly" revised in 1556,[48] just after the publication of the commentaries on Acts, the Gospels, Isaiah, and Genesis, and just before publication of the remaining Old Testament commentaries. Therefore the time spread of our texts is not great. Nonetheless Calvin's way of thinking may have been influenced by the way he encountered the biblical material in his systematic study.

In the last chapter, in the discussion of the commentary on 1 Corinthians 11, it was noted that Calvin understands the whole chapter as dealing with matters of propriety or decorum in the life of the Corinthian congregation. Having established this context for the chapter, Calvin then clarifies that Paul in the opening verses is discussing his view that it is proper for women in public worship to cover their heads and proper for men to uncover theirs. Only as an attempt to interpret this propriety does Paul speak of men as made in the image of God, and not women. Therefore Calvin thinks one should understand this distinction between men and women only as a reflection of the subordinate role of women in marriage and the political order, the realm of human governing *(politia)*, not as a theological statement of woman's inferiority in God's eyes.[49]

In the kingdom of God all differences of sex and social status will be destroyed and spiritual equality made manifest. Even in this world women have absolutely equal access to participation in public worship, the sacraments, and thus the grace of Christ who is Lord of all. Calvin is quite clear that women were created in the image of God as well as men, and that they share in the restoration of that image in the kingdom of Christ, beginning now in the church, equally with men.[50]

> There is neither male nor female, neither great nor small; the one who is most despised, God exalts; the one who is the highest and the most honored, God humiliates. . . . Being members of our Lord Jesus Christ, we are not ashamed at all to receive each other mutually in this concord, and conform ourselves to those who formerly seemed to be below us. All this is indeed certain as to the adoption of God, as to the liberty of the gospel, so that we are able to invoke our God audaciously, as to our being able to depend on his promises, so we do not doubt at all that our heritage is prepared for us in heaven.[51]

All the faithful have in common the reception of the sacraments, to confirm the union with Christ, and the governing of the Holy Spirit, in order to live in virtue. And all form a body where no one is any longer raised up over another.[52]

Nevertheless, Calvin puzzles over the whole discussion because Paul has so clearly stated in 1 Timothy 2:12 that women should not speak in church at all. Therefore it appears to make no sense to discuss whether women should be veiled while prophesying in church. Perhaps Paul refers also to other gatherings, perhaps of women, in private homes,[53] Calvin suggests. A more modern proposal to deal with Calvin's dilemma—that Paul did not write 1 Timothy—does not seem to have occurred to Calvin.

Calvin shows his consciousness of historical context when he deals again in another passage with the question of women's public role in the church. Commenting on 1 Corinthians 14:34–35, where women are instructed to keep silence in the churches and ask instruction of their husbands at home, Calvin begins by explaining that the chattering of women must have been a problem for the Corinthian church, and so Paul therefore forbids them to speak publicly, either to teach or to prophesy. But he immediately qualifies the advice:

> But we should understand this as referring to the situation where things can be done in the regular way, or where the church is well established. For a situation can arise where there is a need of such a kind as calls for a woman to speak. But Paul is confining himself to what is fitting in a properly organized congregation.[54]

He goes on to explain that because the teaching office is one of authority and oversight, it is an office inappropriate for women, who, under the law, are subject to men. Calvin does not comment here on the term "law" in the biblical text. He believes that women have in all ages been excluded from control of public affairs, except that they were for a time allowed to plead in court at Rome. "And common sense dictates that the rule of women is defective and unseemly."[55]

Calvin is aware that not all husbands are capable of teaching their wives what they would like to know. So Paul, not meaning to give the impression of closing the door on women's learning, is not forbidding the women from privately consulting the prophets, if necessary.[56]

> But as [Paul] is discussing the external organization *(externa politia)*
> here, it is enough for his purpose to point out what is indecorous, so
> that the Corinthians might avoid it. However, the discerning reader
> should come to the decision that the things which Paul is dealing with
> here are indifferent, i.e., neither good nor bad; and that none of
> them is forbidden unless it works against decorum and edification.[57]

Commenting on 1 Corinthians 14:37, just after Paul's injunction of women's silence in the church, Calvin raises pertinent questions:

> Truly one could ask here how Paul affirms these things to be precepts
> of the Lord for which there stands no testimony in the Scriptures.
> Then still another question occurs: if they are precepts of the Lord,
> they must of necessity be observed and they bind the conscience. But
> these are administrative arrangements *(ritus politici)* in the observance
> of which there is not such a necessity.[58]

Calvin is sure that Paul is communicating God's counsel for the order of the church at Corinth and elsewhere in external things, something useful for all the children of God and not at all to be neglected; but the advice is not given "so that it will be an inviolable law."[59]

In the conclusion to the whole commentary on 1 Corinthians 14, Calvin reiterates that in discussing the rites of the church, Paul is dealing with external governing or organization *(externa politia)* to preserve decorum and avoid disorder. Paul is not willing to make these instructions binding on people's consciences for the sake of the laws themselves. Unlike tyrannical papal laws, pious laws of the church preserve its discipline and order, and allow freedom with regard to outward rites. But insofar as they derive from the Word they are not to be regarded as mere human traditions, since "they give the impression of being approved, as it were, from the mouth of Christ himself" and help us determine what is right.[60]

In view of Calvin's qualifications of Paul's restrictions on women's role in the church, it should not be surprising that Calvin assumes a greater role for women in the early church than the bare text of the New Testament would oblige him to admit. For example, commenting in Acts 1 on the women's presence in the upper room, Calvin thinks these women may have been the women who had accompanied Christ, but he feels quite sure that the group included the wives of the apostles; for they were later to accompany their husbands and assist them, and they would need heroic fortitude. Calvin believes the apostles awaiting the Spirit would never have deprived their wives of a share in such a blessing, and it is unthinkable that the wives were separated from their husbands at such a time.[61]

The text of Acts 18 recounts simply that when Priscilla and Aquila heard Apollos speaking in the synagogue, "they took him and expounded to him the way of God more accurately." Calvin comments on the generosity of Priscilla and Aquila in taking Apollos aside for private instruction so that he could speak more effectively, for they recognized his great gifts and were not envious of him.

> Again, Apollos was unusually modest, for he allowed himself to be taught and refined, not only by a manual worker, but also by a woman. For he was mighty in Scripture, and far superior to them; but those who could have given the impression of being hardly suitable ministers give him the finishing touches about what makes the Kingdom of Christ complete. We also see that at that time women were not so unacquainted with the Word of God as the Papists wish to have them, since we see that one of the chief teachers of the church was taught by a woman. Yet we must remember what I said, that Priscilla carried out this instruction at home, and within private walls, that she might shake as little as possible the order prescribed by God and by nature.[62]

Calvin also notes the honor that Paul confers upon Priscilla and congratulates Paul on his modesty, "since he does not refuse to have, and is not ashamed to admit that he has, a woman as his associate in the work of the Lord."[63] And Calvin understands Phoebe (Rom. 16:1) to be the bearer of Paul's letter to the Romans and a deacon holding public office.[64]

But in a somewhat different vein Calvin perceives the gifts of prophecy given to the four daughters of Philip to have been recorded in commendation of their father, for this was an extraordinary gift of the Holy Spirit and a sign that his house was well managed and blessed by God. But the gifts of prophecy are also a sign of restoration, to adorn the new reign of Christ through the gospel. Calvin is uncertain how the daughters exercised these gifts so as not to disturb God's order, but he finds it believable that they prophesied at home, or in private, outside the public meeting.[65]

When Calvin is faced with the need to preach on a biblical text like 1 Timothy 2:11–15, where Paul forbids women to teach or have authority over men because Eve was created after Adam and because Eve, not Adam, sinned, it is hardly surprising that Calvin elaborates more than elsewhere on Eve as the source of human sin and on the necessity of women's submission to men as part of the order of nature.

But how does he begin his sermon on this text? Precisely by struggling with the questions it raises. He immediately grants that one could be astonished at Paul's advice, inasmuch as God has indeed sometimes given the charge and the grace of teaching to women: for example, we see that Deborah was not only a prophetess but also governed the people of God. But rather than assume this is a contradiction, we should distinguish between the "common order" which God as a rule wishes to be observed and that which he does in a "strange fashion." For God in making law, which is based on his will, in no way gives up his freedom to act otherwise. Therefore God is free to call a woman to govern or teach. But God usually does so when the situation is "confused" by the sinfulness of men, and God thus uses the calling of a woman to teach or rule over men as a means to chastise and humiliate men, to mock their pretentions.[66]

Among the examples of God's extraordinary action, not regulated in the "common" way, are God's pouring out the Holy Spirit on women as well as men "at the beginning of the gospel," granting the grace of prophecy to the daughters of Philip—though Calvin says here that they were to prophesy among women rather than in the assembly—and the prudence of Abigail which saved the house of Nabal.[67]

But one can also ask, Calvin thinks, whether it is not true that sometimes inferiors rule over superiors in a spiritual fashion, as when pastors teach kings or magistrates. This is possible, he answers, because God has separated the earthly government (*police terrestre*) and the spiritual government (*regime spirituel*) of his church. But in the case of women, Paul explains that "God has established an inviolable rule which should last till the end of the world: since man is created as the head of the woman, and since woman is a part of and like an accessory to man, it is necessary that we follow this direction and that great and small order themselves to it."[68] But Calvin adds immediately that if things go wrong in society, both in public and in private, we can count on God shaming us. God will show us that we are unworthy of his reigning in our midst and will abandon us. "As he says by his prophet Isaiah, that he will make women and little children rule, that is to declare that he will give up his preeminence and that everything will be dissolute and dissipated."[69]

This brings Calvin to the section where Paul adds that women will be saved in bearing children. Calvin understands this passage to be an example of the fact that our Savior in bringing Christian people to humility always then raises them up from their despair. Women who realize in despair that Eve is the cause of the ruin of the world and all humanity, the curse of God and the tyranny of Satan, can discover that all the hardships of pregnancy, birth, and the care of children can be a sacrifice pleasing to God by faith. Paul offers women consolation that their salvation is given them even in the condemnation they feel for their sins.[70] Calvin at length defends the married life against papal teaching of its polluted nature, reassuring women that when they carry out the duties of their office, it is accepted by God, however much it is despised by men. Therefore women should learn to rejoice in their work in the household and family, knowing that God and the angels see and approve. For this work, however much it may seem detestable, is woman's vocation by nature.[71]

Calvin then turns to give men instruction from this text, too. Men are not only to work at their own trade but also to support their wives at home and give them courage, help their wives wherever possible, bear patiently the annoyances of child-rearing and rejoice that this work, too, is an acceptable sacrifice to God. Calvin thinks this spirit will bring about a different order in marriage than what is commonly seen if it is imprinted in the heart.[72]

The chief point which Calvin finds in the text, finally, is that Paul wants to encourage those who faithfully perform what their office requires. Though God is under no obligation because of those works, "our Savior is so liberal and so human that he deigns to look favorably on what they do and approve it, however much they are unworthy of it."[73]

One can see that Paul has in this context led Calvin into the traditional discussion of women as inferior to men, unable to rule according to the common order, both because of Eve's creation after Adam and because Eve was the cause of sin. These are not themes found in the *Institutes*. On the other hand, Calvin is unusually patient in drawing out the possible objections he sees to this teaching, apparently seeing a certain weight in the objections. He makes it clear that the Spirit's freedom in breaking through the common order to call women to teach, prophesy, and rule is not merely a matter of history but can be expected in the future as well, to punish men's unfaithfulness. It appears that what he calls the inviolable order of men ruling over women is inviolable only in the sense that women should not presumptuously seek an office which is not theirs. God is quite free to violate that order by calling women to exercise authority in both the secular and the spiritual realm, and God does so. Calvin also finds this text an occasion to teach the Reformation view of the dignity of marriage and to instruct men on the mutuality required by it, as well as to teach justification by grace alone.

The much briefer Latin commentary on this passage outlines much of the structure of the sermon. But two different questions are raised: the validity of Paul's assumption of male priority by earlier creation in time, and the validity of the view that Adam did not really share in the responsibility for original sin, since Paul holds Eve alone guilty. Calvin admits the weakness of the argument of priority, since John the Baptist preceded Christ yet was of lesser dignity. The next chapter will show that Paul's argument for male supremacy by virtue of prior creation was frequently criticized by Renaissance writers, and Calvin finds little reason to defend it. The issue for Calvin is the purpose of the subsequent creation of Eve, to be Adam's helper; he thinks Paul really intended all the circumstances of the creation to be taken into account. Calvin also rejects even more decisively the argument that Adam was blameless and that only Eve sinned. Paul simply means that Eve was the source of Adam's transgression.[74]

Calvin in the commentary also indicates more clearly that where women have held the role of teaching and prophesying, they did so as called forth by the Holy Spirit, "who is free from all law." But this unusual call by the Spirit "does not conflict with the perpetual and accustomed governance" (*perpetua et usitata politia; communis politia*) to which God wishes us to be bound.[75]

Calvin also introduces here the idea that, although Eve was in some sense already subject to Adam in Paradise and childbearing was then natural to her, since the Fall "her subjection is less befitting a free person (*liberalis*) than before"; "since she had led her husband away from the rule of God, it is appropriate that, deprived of all liberty, she was driven back under the yoke."[76]

The theme of women's teaching as God's rebuke to unfaithful men can also be found elsewhere—for example, in the Gospel accounts of the passion and resurrection. Calvin in preaching on Matthew 27 comments concerning the women at the cross:

> If here men and their magnanimity had been spoken of, and that they had followed our Lord Jesus Christ to the death, one would take that as a natural thing. But when the women are led by the Spirit of God, and there is in them more audacity than in men, even those who had been elected to publish the gospel in all the world, in that let us recognize that God has worked and that it is to him that the praise should be attributed. . . . Nevertheless this is not to say that there were not also men. But the intention of the Holy Spirit has been to put here before our eyes such a mirror that we may know that it is God who led these women by the power of his Holy Spirit and willed to declare his power and his grace, choosing thus instruments feeble according to the world.[77]

Christ's choosing to reveal his resurrection first to the women rather than to the disciples may at first seem strange, Calvin comments in the French sermons, but Christ doubtless wanted to punish the disciples because they had fled, by sending women to teach them. But this "ordaining" of women as teachers was not a rigorous punishment but a "mild correction." The lesson Christ teaches here is that God ordains those who seem good to him as his witnesses; and one should not refuse to receive their testimony, even if they seem unlikely choices by the world's standards.[78]

Calvin's Latin commentary on the Synoptic accounts of the resurrection seems to have a somewhat different tone. The element of incongruity of women's teaching is much less marked here, and Calvin freely acknowledges that the apostolic mandate was indeed given to the women at the tomb for a brief time.

> [Christ] even gave them the message of the gospel for the apostles, in order to make them the teachers of the apostles: this in the first place was a rebuke to the listlessness of the apostles, who were lying all but dead of fright where the women were anxiously hurrying to the tomb and thereby earned no common reward. . . . [Pardoning their mistaken intent to anoint the body, Christ] deemed them worthy of singular honor, giving over to them the apostolic mandate taken away from the men for a short time.[79]

Calvin finds this an example of God's choosing the weak things of the world to humiliate the loftiness of the flesh.[80] And he credits the women in their mission to the apostles with reuniting and restoring the scattered church.[81]

In his commentary on John 20, Calvin sees Mary Magdalene's word of recognition, "Rabboni," as depicting for us the "image of our calling."[82] Mary professed herself to be a disciple of Christ and obeyed her teacher by going to the assembled disciples to tell them of the resurrection. They by their unfaithfulness "were worthy not only of women as teachers, but also oxen and asses. . . . This is still a mild and gentle punishment when Christ thus sent away the disciples to the school of women, in order that he might through the women call the disciples to himself."[83]

Though recognizing that John's account speaks only of Mary Magdalene, Calvin in his commentary on John 20 harmonizes this account with the Synoptic ones and continues to talk of the "women" witnesses of the resurrection who were given by Christ's inestimable goodness such a fundamental role in our salvation. But at the same time he warns that this was an extraordinary and almost "accidental" occurrence. Though the women were commanded to announce the news to the apostles, they did not do this as "apostles." And Calvin immediately clarifies that he is refuting those who claim by this text the right of women to baptize. But he returns to the marvelous grace shown here to the women in making them on that occasion teachers of the apostles, especially to Mary Magdalene, formerly captive of seven demons, whom Christ has raised up from the lowest depths to a place above the heavens. If anyone should object that the women were just as carnal and stupid as the apostles, Calvin replies that the choice between the women and the apostles is not for us, but rather for the Judge, to decide.[84]

In a similar way Calvin comments on the amazement of the disciples that Jesus talked with the woman at the well. The proper response to make when one finds something in the words or works of God or Christ inconsistent with one's understanding is to be silent modestly until what is hidden is disclosed from heaven.[85] This woman called others to come and hear Jesus but did not assume for herself the role of teacher. So Calvin commends her for her alacrity in sharing her new faith with others, which he believes is a mark of true faith.[86]

Finally Calvin's commentary on Genesis must be examined to see how he understands the place of woman in Paradise. Since he had already worked his way through the biblical texts discussed, before publishing the Genesis commentary, one can be sure that he has Paul's teaching clearly in mind.

Commenting on Genesis 1:27, "So God created a human being in his own image, in the image of God he created the person; male and female he created them," Calvin points out that God here "commends the conjugal bond by which the community of the human race is fostered."[87] It is as if God had called the man only "half a human being," and thus had added to the man a female companion, "so that both might be one," which, Calvin thinks, is more clearly expressed in Genesis 2.[88]

Here there is no hint in Calvin's comments of any subjection of the woman to the man. Rather, Calvin sees the whole human being as requiring both male and female, and the woman is a companion.

But just prior to this passage, in commenting on Genesis 1:26 about the image and likeness of God, Calvin adds to the discussion:

> Indeed this difficulty is also to be resolved: why Paul denies that woman is the image of God, inasmuch as Moses honors both sexes indiscriminately with this title. The solution briefly stated is that Paul there touches upon only the domestic status. Thus he restricts the image of God to the dominion (*principatum*) in which the man is pre-eminent over the woman; and he certainly does not mean anything other than that he is superior in the degree of honor.[89]

Calvin regards Genesis 2 as explaining Genesis 1 more fully. Therefore he harmonizes it with what had gone before. Adam in 2:16 has already been made governor of the world, subject only to God, before Eve is created.[90] Now in 2:18 the text describes the woman to be created as a helper. Calvin still defends woman as created in the image of God, though he adds, "although in the second degree";[91] and he concludes that the order of nature makes it proper for woman to be man's helper. He specifically refutes the notion that woman is merely a necessary evil, however, preferring God's word that she is a companion and associate to man,[92] made "equal" to him.[93]

Calvin thinks Eve was not easy for the serpent to seduce into evil;[94] nonetheless both Adam and Eve fell into unfaithfulness, then ambition, pride, and ingratitude.[95] Even since the Fall men and women have a mutual obligation to one another, but the task set before them is made more difficult than before.[96] Eve was punished not only by the pain of childbearing but also by a new sort of subjection to her husband. Before, her subjection had been appropriate to a free person (*liberalis*) and not at all hard; now she was cast into bondage.[97]

The reader senses that Calvin remains troubled by Paul's way of dealing with Eve. He regularly refutes an interpretation of Paul that would deny woman's share in the image of God; he points out that Paul in many passages teaches that Adam sinned along with Eve; but in the end his reading of the second chapter of Genesis represents an attempt to harmonize that account with the first chapter and with Paul. And so Eve's subjection predates the Fall, and Eve's share in the image of God is not entirely equal.

Calvin continues to struggle with this understanding of inequality between male and female in his sermon on Job 3:3, where Job in his misery curses the day of his birth, saying, "Let the day perish wherein I was born, and the night which said, 'A man-child is conceived.' " Calvin begins by insisting on the gratitude all persons should have for their creation in the image of God, leading them to bless the day of their birth.[98] But he thinks Job must have wanted to spite God especially by the reference to a male child, because in human nature men are preferred over women; God has given the man dignity and preeminence over the woman, as Paul says in 1 Corinthians 11:7. "It is true that the image of God is well imprinted on every person; but so is it true that the woman is inferior to man. It is necessary that we go along with these degrees which God has instituted in the order of nature."[99] Therefore, though God is glorified in every birth, he is especially glorified in the birth of a male child. Nonetheless Christians should receive whatever child is born to them as God's choice of what is good for them, rejoicing in the birth of boys but not rejecting their daughters. God sometimes punishes parents who are too eager for boys for selfish reasons. Though the woman should be subject to man, she was also created to be a companion to him and should not be treated contemptuously. "God created and formed us and now continues the human race by men and by women; but it is so that we may live together with a common accord, knowing that there is a communal bond which God has consecrated between us as inviolable."[100]

Since marriage certainly is one of the realms where Calvin sees man as the head of the woman, following biblical teaching, it is important to note that it is Calvin's careful reading of the Bible which also persuades him that women have certain grounds for genuine equality in marriage. For example, he understands Paul's call for mutuality between husband and wife in 1 Corinthians 7:3–5 to extend beyond conjugal rights. But Calvin then asks concerning conjugal rights why the apostle makes man and woman "equal partners and does not demand obedience and subjection from the wife? . . . Husband and wife . . . have different rights and duties in other things, but in the preservation of married faithfulness they are on an equal footing."[101] Calvin also sees in Matthew 19:9 an obligation to give wives and husbands equal right to divorce. In fact Geneva's divorce laws were altered in this direction. Biéler comments:

> According to the social ethic of Calvin, the presence in a society of Christians living in conformity to the norms of the gospel—in the spiritual liberty which the Christ offers to them—creates pressure on the juridical structures which tend to draw together the political law, valid for all, with Christian ethics, in force in the church.[102]

Our reading of Calvin would suggest several conclusions about his view of women's place in the church and society.

1. In the successive editions of the *Institutes* Calvin evidences exceedingly little explicit positive support for the traditional general subordination of women. One can deduce that he assumes it from his use once of the image of the obedient bride and from the recognition he gives subordination by asserting in the context of the image of God that subordination is limited to the realm of human governance. This traditional cultural pattern of subordination of women is reinforced by his regular use of biblical imagery of God or Christ as husband of the church, or of the people of God as his bride, imagery where the human bride is clearly subordinate.[103]

But explicitly Calvin argues in the context of Christian freedom that both Paul's teaching about the necessity for women to be veiled, presumably both in church and society, and Paul's command for women to be silent in the church should be understood in the context of human governance; therefore both should be received as respected advice but not as eternal law that binds the conscience. Both could be adapted to changing circumstances for the edification of the church. Calvin also teaches that women undertook public ministry in the early church as deacons.

2. The commentary and sermons on 1 Corinthians explicitly echo the understanding of the *Institutes*. Calvin goes far beyond what the text would require to insist on placing Paul's limitation on women's freedom in the context of human governance, not divine and eternal law.

The other commentaries are much less explicit about this context of order. Calvin freely acknowledges that according to the biblical record, women did at times rule, teach, and prophesy, called by the Spirit, though he believes the Bible is generally understood by tradition to deny them those roles. But he tends to explain this in the later commentaries more as a late medieval theologian might do, as an example of miracle where God's freedom breaks through the order God has created. Nonetheless, the fact that he retains his consistent teaching in the *Institutes* on Christian freedom in regard to Paul's advice suggests that we should continue to read the other commentaries in that context also. Calvin appears to be very much aware that women's role in church and society is being debated, and he struggles far more than one might expect with the problems raised by biblical texts that teach women's public subordination in the church. Nonetheless in the commentaries Calvin clearly and explicitly approves a social order where men exercise authority over women, and he reveals his own traditional feelings that women are inferior to men.

3. Calvin seems haunted by 1 Corinthians 11:7 and Paul's apparent teaching there that only men are made in the image of God. Again and again in various contexts Calvin rejects the most obvious interpretation in favor of his own view that Paul intends such restriction of women's dignity to apply only to the realm of human governance and that women really are made in the image of God in the theological sense. Calvin rightly perceives that this text is a key one for the traditional theological teaching of women's subordination to men. Whatever modern exegetes might think of Calvin's treatment of this admittedly very difficult text, we note that Calvin has to his own satisfaction transformed this text from one of the foundation stones of a theological justification of women's subordination into theological support for women's greater freedom in the church at some future time.

4. Calvin's personal judgment seems to be that Geneva in the sixteenth century would be as scandalized by women in public roles of authority in either church or state as Paul imagined the first-century society would be. Since he regarded major social upheaval as a great danger to civilization, he was very reluctant to recommend revolutionary social change of any sort unless required by the Word of God. Given his concern for the consciences of his brothers, who would indeed be greatly offended by women in authority, and given his own prejudices, he seems generally content to tolerate and perpetuate the social subordination of women both in church and society as a style of decorum approved by the Bible.

Nonetheless it is apparent that Calvin is engaged in a not entirely subtle process of consciousness-raising, helping Genevans to understand that God's word properly understood does not forbid women to serve in roles of authority in the church, that God by the Holy Spirit has in fact repeatedly called women into such roles and probably will again. In the next chapter, aspects of Calvin's context that support such a view will be explored. Calvin seems very eager to point out that even Paul, who had been traditionally understood to forbid women to have public roles of authority over men, in fact himself had women associates in his work, some of whom served in the public office of deacon. Still, Calvin's division of the biblical deacon's office into two parts has the effect of lessening the authoritative role of women in that office.

5. Despite all that has been said about the care with which he has worked out the theological distinction between what is required by the gospel and the whole realm of civil and church law, which is caught up in changing culture and adaptable according to current needs, and over against which the Christian's conscience is free, Calvin seems occasionally to worry about the consequences of his position for the authority of the whole Bible. By making a distinction between the authority of what Christ has taught and the advice Paul has given, Calvin might appear to relativize the authority of the epistles; he might be accused of having created a "canon within a canon."[104]

Calvin seems perfectly comfortable with his position so long as he dialogues with Paul about what is "natural" with regard to men's hats and the length of men's hair. He does not appear distressed to admit Paul's ethnocentrism on these points or to approve Genevan dissent.[105]

In principle Calvin is prepared to argue that Paul's view of women's subordination as "natural" falls precisely into the same category as Paul's view that long hair on men goes against the order of nature, that theologically the biblical restrictions he finds on women's freedom in church and society are relative, caught up with changing circumstances, while women's freedom in the kingdom of God is absolute. Yet at that point he several times shows his discomfort with that position; he feels the need to point out that church decorum should be patterned after the biblical view of proper order, and that Paul's advice, because it is recorded in Scripture, lends the tradition of women's subordination in the church a kind of divine approval which should not be lightly disregarded. Still Calvin is trying very hard to be faithful to the Reformation view that Christian consciences have been radically freed by the gospel from all servitude to such traditions.

It is very interesting that in these explicit discussions of freedom in order Calvin never claims Christ's teaching or example as justification for women's subordination in the church but deals only with Paul's advice and the order of creation.

There remain some questions which should still be posed to

Calvin within his own system—questions for which I have been unable to find answers. For example, given Calvin's view of the inbreaking of the kingdom in the church, why does he not distinguish more sharply between church and state where decorum is concerned? One would think that the equality of the kingdom would justify more radical change in decorum in the church than in the society at large. But his approval of the reign of contemporary queens seems to suggest just the opposite.[106] Since queens can be tolerated because the populace is accustomed to women rulers and is not scandalized, how could the church become accustomed to women leaders so that they would no longer be seen as scandalous?

How would Calvin and the Genevan church decide whether a woman who claimed to be led by the Spirit of God to undertake extraordinary leadership in the church was in fact called by God or was merely a presumptuous and rebellious woman, unwilling to bear the yoke patiently? Though in principle Calvin believes the Spirit will raise up women as leaders, in practice Calvin apparently cites no cases of such calling by the Spirit since the New Testament.

Calvin's way of dealing theologically with the public role of women is an unusual and intriguing one for the sixteenth century, probably genuinely innovative. It is clear that Calvin was courageous enough to struggle with what he perceived to be a very thorny problem in order to protect the Reformation doctrine of Christian freedom when many before and even after him have disposed of the matter far more simply by merely quoting the apostle Paul.

Nevertheless, it is unlikely that Calvin's theological labor produced any practical consequences at all for women's public roles in the church. He declined to press for changes in the church to permit women's leadership in his own day. In the absence of institutional change to call attention to his views, his theological vision of freedom went unnoticed, and women's subordinate status in the church remained the same for another three hundred and fifty years.

4
Women's Freedom in Church Order: Calvin in the Medieval and Renaissance Context

The reader of Calvin is hardly in a position to evaluate his point of view without having some sense of the ways in which he merely echoes the thought and experience of his day and the ways in which he represents a unique voice. Therefore the context in which to interpret Calvin's understanding of the freedom of women in church order must be explored.

But this is no easy task, for the sixteenth century was a time of intellectual upheaval and social change. In different classes of society, different geographical regions, and different theological communities, widely divergent views of the ideal role for women and very different experiences of real women's roles in church and society can be found. Sorting out these differences is challenging contemporary historians to careful and patient analysis of a variety of sources. For example, we can mention Natalie Davis's[1] studies of women of different classes in various French cities and Ruth Kelso's[2] description of the ideal life of noblewomen. Respected myths like that of the equality of Italian noblewomen of the Renaissance to men are being revised today.[3] So no simple and easy summary is possible.

Only those aspects of the medieval and Renaissance context which seem to touch most directly on Calvin's own discussions of women's role laid out in the last chapter have been selected for inclusion in this chapter. Nevertheless, three quite general paradoxes must be pointed out.

1. Though a few women exercised very considerable influence in sixteenth-century society, most women had relatively little control over their own lives. For example, the queens of England,

especially Elizabeth, and Marguerite of Austria come to mind quickly as influential women. Also in France there was a remarkable group of women at court during the middle third of the century, playing important political roles: Louise of Savoy, mother of Francis I; Marguerite of Angoulême, sister of Francis I, and her daughter, Jeanne d'Albret, both queens of Navarre;[4] Michelle de Saubonne, known as Madame de Soubise, *gouvernante* of Renée de France, and Renée herself, who became the Duchess of Ferrara;[5] and the diplomats of the civil wars: the Comtesse de Roye and the Marquise de Rothelin, along with Jeanne d'Albret.[6] A Renaissance enthusiast may call this the "century of illustrious women."[7] But the public power of such women remains quite exceptional in the period.

2. The sources repeatedly assert that women's place is in the home, under the authority of fathers or husbands; the only legitimate alternative is the convent for Catholic women. Yet some social historians today are suggesting that in fact a pattern was emerging in the fifteenth and sixteenth centuries where most people married late, and very large numbers never married at all. Eric Midelfort describes this as "one of the most profound demographic changes that Europe ever experienced."[8] He estimates that men were marrying for the first time at 25 to 30, women at 23 to 27 years of age; the proportion of persons remaining single rose from about 5 to possibly 20 percent, much higher in some places.

Repeated emphasis, therefore, on the importance of subordination of women in the sixteenth century would seem to be only partly a matter of mere traditional teaching; it may be also partly a response to the threat of social change which is disrupting traditional patterns of life. Much more information is needed, however, before one can be certain of the nature and impact of this phenomenon.

3. Paeans of praise for women arise from Renaissance writers of the period, mostly men; and some of this praise would probably be called extravagant even in the twentieth century. Nonetheless the sixteenth century is also an age of misogyny, if one reads its literature. Possibly the level of vituperation was even higher than in previous centuries.[9]

Keeping these paradoxes in mind may help to maintain some perspective in listening to the sources. Such ambivalent attitudes are not uncommon in periods of great social change.

It is also important to remember that the Reformation period is encircled by great epidemics of witch-hunting, which were at their peak in the fifteenth through the seventeenth centuries. The three paradoxes above surely have some bearing on this phenomenon, since on the whole during this period women were far more widely suspected of witchcraft than men—especially single women[10]—and since judges of witchcraft were men. One cannot ignore the consequent impact of the hysteria of witchcraft trials on the relations between men and women at this time.

The sixteenth century continued enthusiastically the late medieval *querelle des femmes* in humanistic circles of Europe, particularly in France, i.e., the great literary debate ("quarrel") mostly carried on by men about the superiority or inferiority of women; now it appeared that the women might be winning.[11] While some writers poked fun at women's foibles and some ridiculed and vilified women, others like Henry Cornelius Agrippa of Nettesheim engaged in lyrical exaltation of women over men, an exaltation that most commentators find not entirely free of sarcasm.

Agrippa in his famed *Declamation on the Nobility and Excellence of the Feminine Sex* of 1509 denies any inherent inferiority of women with respect to the nature of the soul, the hope of glory, mind, body, or speech, but insists that both have equal dignity and innate liberty. Yet women are even superior in some ways, Agrippa suggests; for example, they were made by God in Paradise with the angels, whereas Adam was created outside Paradise in a field with the animals.[12] Eve's superiority is shown by her name, meaning life, whereas the name Adam means earth.[13] As the last of all that God created, Eve is the crowning achievement of God, the most perfect work of God.[14] Original sin is to be traced to Adam, not Eve; and Christ, to save sinful humanity, was made human in the more lowly male sex from which sin came forth; he was incarnated by means of a woman, not a man. Every male priest in representing Christ in fact represents the man Adam, the first sinner.[15] The canon in church law which specifies that woman is not made in the image of God is to be understood as meaning that woman is not made in the bodily likeness of Christ.[16] Christ was betrayed, crucified, and abandoned only by men, whereas women remained at the cross, came to the empty tomb, and were witnesses to the resurrection.[17]

Agrippa laments eloquently the loss of the freedom originally given woman by the law of God and of nature; this freedom is forbidden to her by men's tyrannical laws, abolished by custom, and extinguished by education. She is shut up in the household from the time of her birth and forbidden public duties. She is not permitted to preach the word of God, though the Holy Scriptures expressly promise that the Spirit will be poured out on women and they will prophesy (Joel 2:28–29). In the apostolic age Anna, the daughters of Philip, and Priscilla taught publicly. Against the men who arrogate religious authority for themselves in their tyrannical treatment of women by ceaselessly proclaiming the curse of Eve and Paul's advice for women to be submissive and silent in church, Agrippa cites biblical texts proclaiming that Christ has taken away the curse, that God is no respecter of persons, and that in Christ there is neither male nor female but a new person.[18]

Though much of the turning of traditional texts and examples of women's subjection to their exaltation is a matter of argumentation, at least once Agrippa actually transforms the text. For example, he proclaims that Scripture declares that the iniquity of a woman is far better regarded than a beneficent man. In fact, Ecclesiasticus 42:14 says the opposite: "A man's wickedness is better than a beneficent woman." One interpreter, Émile Telle, suggests this particular parody of Scripture may explain Calvin's hostile comment about Agrippa as having "foolishly scorned the Scripture."[19] But since Calvin did not recognize the canonicity of the Apocrypha, of which Ecclesiasticus is a part, he is more likely to be complaining about the whole theological perspective than this particular text.

We have chosen Agrippa as an example, rather than other humanists with similar ideas, because we can connect him to Calvin directly. Calvin certainly knew Agrippa from his writings, but probably also from his local reputation in Geneva, where Agrippa resided briefly in the early 1520s,[20] before Calvin arrived. Because Agrippa had many friends among those who joined the Reformation, and because he so regularly articulated humanistic criticism of Catholicism, some scholars have argued that he should be seen as a sort of unconfessed Protestant. This seems very unlikely, however.[21] Calvin emphasizes his lack of reverence despite his learning: "While he magnificently extols the eternity of the word of God, he scurrilously ridicules the prophets and the apostles and thus obliquely mocks the word of God."[22]

Yet there are some indications Calvin has heard the humanistic challenges to traditional doctrine that Agrippa and others were making. It was noted in the last chapter, for example, that Calvin recognizes the weakness of Paul's argument in 1 Timothy for male supremacy on the basis that Adam was created prior to Eve.[23] And the next chapter will show that Calvin is very careful to clarify that the pouring out of the Spirit prophesied by Joel should not be equated with permission to preach,[24] in contrast to Agrippa's conclusion that it should.

Another figure in the *querelle des femmes* literature of the time who is much more closely related to Calvin is Marguerite of Angoulême, queen of Navarre and sister of Francis I, king of France. Marguerite was a highly educated Renaissance woman, author of religious and secular poetry and prose. She was also at the center of that remarkable group of French noblewomen at court with very considerable political influence, and with whom Calvin had considerable contact. These relationships will be further discussed in the next chapter. Marguerite, like Calvin in his student days, was strongly attracted to the movement of reforming biblical humanism in France. During the time that Calvin was a part of this movement, she protected its representatives when they were threatened by conservative religious and political forces. Marguerite read and translated some portions of Luther, but she never openly espoused the Reformation when Protestantism became clearly distinguished in France from reforming Catholic humanism.[25]

Marguerite's religious poetry, often quite mystical, can be shown to reflect some Lutheran themes. Her poem "Mirror of the Sinful Soul" was in fact the object of an official theological investigation of its orthodoxy; Marguerite replied with a satirical playlet, "The Inquisitor."[26] The poem, however, was widely read and even translated into English prose by Elizabeth of England, then an eleven-year-old princess.[27]

Modern literary critics are much more impressed by the style of Marguerite's novels than her poetry.[28] And it is in the novels especially that we find expressions of her less than traditional views of women's role. A modern commentator, Telle, considers Marguerite's position far more moderate than that of Agrippa, more conscious of the weaknesses of both sexes and more focused on their complementarity.[29] But he is especially interested in the way Marguerite, like other Renaissance figures such as Agrippa, Erasmus, and Postel, turns the authority of the apostle Paul to the support of women's dignity rather than their degradation. On the one hand a character from Marguerite's writing can admit that man is "head" of the woman, but on the other hand the man's authority is immediately qualified. "It is reasonable that man governs us as our head, but not that he abandons us or treats us badly."[30] In another passage from the *Heptaméron* Marguerite includes a sparring match between men and women about women's virtues. A woman, Oisille, replies:

> You are praising the graces of our Lord, for to tell the truth, all virtue comes from him; but it is necessary to make the judgment that as

little favors the man in the work of God as the woman, for neither one by the heart and will does anything except plant, and God alone gives the increase.

If you have indeed read Scripture well, says Saffredent (who does not wish to admit that the man is less virtuous than the woman), St. Paul says that Apollo planted and he watered; but he does not say at all that women have put their hands to the work of God.

You would like to follow, says Parlamente, the opinion of wicked men who take a passage of Scripture for themselves and leave behind the one which is the opposite of it. If you have read St. Paul all the way to the end, you will find that he commends himself to the ladies who have worked very hard with him in the gospel.[31]

Marguerite stands in a tradition of women defenders of women in the *querelle des femmes*. Probably the first and best known is Christine de Pizan, writing in the early fifteenth century in France and squarely attacking the misogyny of male writers.[32] We have focused on Marguerite because of her clear connection with Calvin.

Perhaps the most radical supporter of women in this context is Guillaume Postel. In his work of 1553, *The Very Marvelous Victories of the Women of the New World,* he sets out in mystical fashion to prove that women should be the rulers of both the old world, Europe and the Orient, and the newly discovered Americas. A new incarnation of the Holy Spirit in a woman will inaugurate a new era of political and religious harmony.[33] The female "psychosomatic state is more in harmony with the sublunary world than is the male's."[34] I have found no specific response of Calvin's to this work of Postel's. But in response to other works, Calvin complains of Postel as one who in scorn wants to invent a new religion.[35]

Even among Renaissance writers far more conservative in their estimate of women's place in society than Postel there is a strong current of concern about the need for improvement of women's education. Erasmus hoped "even the lowliest women" would read the Gospels and the epistles of Paul. Thomas More saw that his daughters as well as his son learned Latin, Greek, logic, theology, philosophy, mathematics, and astronomy. His oldest daughter, Margaret, came to be recognized as a scholar, translating Erasmus' theological work into English.[36] These and other humanists tended to blame the restricted conditions of women's lives and their lack of education rather than their innate constitutions for the weaknesses they exhibited and believed reform of piety would require reform of education as well.[37]

At the other end of the spectrum of views on women's status is the debate beginning late in the sixteenth century as to whether women are even human. An anonymous treatise now attributed to Acidalius appeared in central Germany satirizing contemporary Socinian dissent from the orthodox doctrine of Christ's divinity, arguing that the biblical record certainly calls Christ God but the Bible nowhere proves women are human. The author offers to give up his objections to women as human if the Socinians will give up their objections to the divinity of Christ.[38]

Among the arguments made against women's humanity are the lack of clear biblical statements about their being made in God's image, the absence of women's names in biblical genealogies, and the use of *vir* (a male person) and not *homo* (a human being) for the saved in Ephesians 4:13.[39] Though the book of Acts mentions baptisms of women, that does not prove they were human, since in the Catholic Church bells were also baptized, the author claims.[40]

Ian Maclean believes that this satire is directed against the "bibliolatry" of the Anabaptists; "indeed it is more informative about the function of intellectual jokes in the Renaissance than about women."[41] Nonetheless the treatise was debated at least till 1688, when the last academic trial on the question was held in Wittenberg; the two chief documents in the debate, the treatise by Acidalius and the refutation by Gediccus, were reprinted as late as 1766 in Paris. The theological faculties of Wittenberg and Leipzig were especially eager to refute the claim that women are not human.[42] So the satire was not universally perceived to be a joke at the time, or at least not a tolerably tasteful joke. Fleischer concludes that while Acidalius' original treatise reflects humanist ambivalence about women reflected in the *querelle des femmes* literature, Lutherans like Gediccus had developed a new sensitivity about the dignity of women that made it impossible for them to continue to laugh at the traditional satire demeaning women.[43]

Did the church ever in fact try to claim that women are not human? It seems that the only time the question had been raised previously was at the second Council of Mâcon in Gaul in 585, and the remembrance of that council plays a role in the sixteenth-century controversy.[44] Even nineteenth- and twentieth-century writers sometimes refer to a debate on the subject that is supposed to have taken place there.[45] One account alleges that there was serious discussion of whether women have souls and that the women's supporters won by only one vote.[46] However, the learned student of the great councils, Hefele, declares that no official record of such a debate can be found. No canon of the council deals with the matter.[47] The only evidence he can point to is an account by Gregory of Tours, a contemporary historian, of an incident at the Council when a bishop came forward to assert that a woman could not be called *homo,* a human being.

> However, he accepted the reasonings of the other bishops and did not press his case: for the holy book of the Old Testament tells us that in the beginning, when God created humankind, "Male and female created he them . . . ," yet of both he used the word *homo.* Similarly our Lord Jesus Christ is called the Son of Man, although he was the son of the Virgin, . . . of a woman. . . . They supported their argument with many other references, and he said no more.[48]

Hefele seems inclined to the interpretations of this episode that make of it a grammatical issue concerning the gender of the word *homo* rather than a theological issue concerning the humanity of women.[49] In any case Gregory of Tours regards the bishop as an isolated questioner who was quickly silenced by the unanimous insistence of his peers that women can properly be spoken of as *homines,* human beings.

Though the church may have been quite clear that women were human, theologians were not at all clear that women were the equals of men. From the time of the Fathers right through the period of the Renaissance and the Reformation, theologians believed that women were created by God to be subordinate to men by the order of nature. It was especially Augustine and Thomas who shaped the view of the Western church, and their views on women's subordination have been carefully studied by Kari Børresen.

Augustine deals with the differences between the two stories of human creation in Genesis 1 and 2 by differentiating two aspects of creation. In Genesis 1 we see the creation of Adam and Eve from the *rationes seminales* (seminal reasons). This *informatio* is simultaneous for Adam and Eve; therefore both have the same relation to God and are equally *homo,* human. But in Genesis 2 we see the *conformatio* of Adam and Eve by which their bodies were created in time; first Adam was created *vir,* a man, then Eve afterward as *femina,* a woman. Therefore their relation to each other as the archetypal couple is determined by their sexual distinction and by Eve's having been created later in time and being dependent on Adam for her body. Augustine can imagine no other reason for God to have given Adam a female helper than the purpose of procreation; Eve is needed as the passive recipient of Adam's seed in procreation. All these factors determine her generally subordinate relation to Adam. Yet Augustine stresses Eve's likeness to Adam, her fundamental humanness, which distinguishes both

Adam and Eve from all other created beings. He understands the creation of Eve from Adam's side as an important symbol of the fact that all human beings come from a single source; this common origin should help to promote human unity. Yet though Eve's body is derived from Adam's, her soul is not said by Scripture to be dependent on Adam's soul: Adam calls her "flesh of my flesh" but not "soul of my soul."[50] Here again one sees a spiritual equality of men and women.

How then does Augustine deal with Paul's discussions of the image of God in 1 Corinthians 11, where Paul says that man is "the image and glory of God; but woman is the glory of man"? First of all, men and women both possess a rational soul, that which is peculiar to humanity among the creatures and is the fundamental mark of the image of God. Faced with the need to reconcile Genesis 1 with 1 Corinthians 11, Augustine is very clear from Genesis 1 that women do indeed possess the image of God in their souls, which are asexual. But he resorts to allegory to explain the meaning of Paul's comment. Within the human soul there exist two elements, one masculine, devoting itself to contemplation of eternal truths, and one feminine, providing for earthly needs. Paul is understood to be referring to this distinction of roles within the human soul. Man in his maleness reflects the superior masculine element of the soul in a way woman in her femaleness does not. So there is a correspondence between men's souls and their exterior humanness while there is, rather, duality for women between their souls and their exterior humanness.[51]

In his discussions of the Trinity, Augustine explains this slightly differently:

> According to Genesis, human nature as such has been made to the image of God, a nature which exists in both sexes and which does not allow of our setting woman aside when it comes to understanding what the image of God is. . . . The wife with her husband is the image of God, so that the totality of this human substance forms a single image; but when woman is considered as man's helpmate, a state which belongs to her alone, she is not the image of God. By contrast, man is the image of God by being solely what he is, an image so perfect, so whole, that when woman is joined with him it makes only one image.[52]

Though woman is thus in a very fundamental way subordinate to man, she can nonetheless contemplate divine truths and take inspiration from them, and the image of God deformed by sin can be renewed through baptism. Women of faith will be resurrected after death with women's bodies, since the differentiation of the sexes stems from God's creation, not from sin. Augustine struggles with the interpretation of "the perfect man" *(vir perfectus)* of Ephesians 4:13, denying that *vir* here should be understood solely in the sense of the male sex. *Vir* should be taken as *homo*, a human being, including women who fear the Lord. Because procreation is no longer needed in the resurrected state, women's status as ancillary and subordinate will be superseded.[53]

Women therefore experience a greater disjunction between their spiritual and their corporeal existence only in this earthly life. In this world they must live in subordination to men. Augustine recognizes one exception in acknowledging that Paul grants women equality in conjugal rights to protect the marriage from adultery. And he struggles in the same vein with women's rights to separate or divorce in case of adultery.[54] Augustine acknowledges one other exception in the case of the virgins, and to a somewhat lesser extent, widows. Women who renounce marriage in order to devote themselves entirely to spiritual fruitfulness escape to the greatest extent possible in this life from the subordination to men which is linked to procreation; and they anticipate in part the equality all women will experience in the resurrected state.[55] For after the resurrection rewards will be based on individual gifts of grace and merit, not influenced by sex.[56]

Thomas Aquinas was of course a very serious student of Augustine, and his view of women's relation to men is deeply influenced by Augustine. He agrees that women possess human souls, but also that woman's creation after man in time and her ancillary role, defined very largely in terms of her help in procreation of the species through passive reception of male seed and nurturing the child, demand her subordination to men in this life. He also agrees that women may receive all sacraments except that of Holy Orders, and that after death women will be raised as women but without the subordination of this life. Sex will not enter into the determination of rewards after death. And he agrees that virginity is the mode of life in this world that most approximates the spiritual equality that will exist after death.[57] By renouncing her most specifically female nature the virgin most nearly loses her subordination.

Yet Thomas's different anthropology, more Aristotelian than Platonic, gives some special emphases to his view. First, Augustine's distinction between *informatio* and *conformatio* becomes problematic because of the unity of soul and body. Therefore, for Thomas, Eve's soul and body are both created after that of Adam in time.[58]

God created woman for the good purpose of procreation, and thus in general woman's nature is not lacking. But an individual woman's nature is that of a defective male, as Aristotle believed.

> For the active power which is found in the male seed is designed to produce something which has like perfection to the male sex, but if a girl is begotten, this is the result of a weakness in the active power or of some evil inclination in the matter, or even of some change brought about from outside, like the south wind which is humid.[59]

Since woman is human, she shares the natural capacity of all humans to use the rational soul to know and love God and thus can be said to be made in the image of God. But there is a secondary sense in which there is a difference between men and women:

> The image of God exists in man *(vir)* in a way that is not found in woman: as a matter of fact, man is the beginning and end of woman as God is the beginning and end of all creation. Once when the Apostle had said "man is the image and glory of God whilst woman is the glory of man," he showed why he had said that, by adding: "It was not man who was taken from woman, but woman from man, and man was not created for woman, but woman was created for man."[60]

Thomas thinks the image of God may be more perfect in man than woman just as there is a difference in perfection between higher and lower angels, though he notes that women and men belong to the same species whereas the angels represent different species.[61] Insofar as the image of God is seen as conforming with grace and glory, there is no distinction between men and women. For the distinctions of sex have to do only with corporeal life.[62]

Thomas, like Augustine, recognizes a certain equivalence in marriage between husband and wife in the matter of conjugal rights, but he appears to restrict that equality somewhat more than Augustine.[63] Beyond this very precisely limited equality, women are subordinate to their husbands.

Thomas recognizes one other sort of equality, that of a spiritual sort in this life: God is free to give women the gifts of teaching or prophecy. These gifts relate to the spiritual life, where distinctions of sex do not apply. Nonetheless, these gifts are to be exercised in privacy, not publicly in the church. Regardless of spiritual gifts, no woman may be ordained to the priesthood, because by her very physical nature she is incapable of signifying superiority of rank.[64] The women to whom Christ appeared at the tomb after his resurrection overcame the curse put on Eve and anticipated the glory of the life to come in rising above their subordinate status.

But they were not permitted to proclaim the resurrection publicly; they merely informed the apostles.[65]

The subordination proper to woman's nature is affirmed by Thomas to be part of the original order of creation, not the result of the Fall.

> Subjection is of two kinds; one is that of slavery, in which the ruler manages the subject for his own advantage, and this sort of subjection came after sin. But the other kind of subjection is domestic or civil, in which the ruler manages his subjects for *their* advantage and benefit. And this sort of subjection would have obtained even before sin. For the human group would have lacked the benefit of order had some of its members not been governed by others who were wiser. Such is the subjection in which woman is by nature subordinate to man, because the power of rational discernment is by nature stronger in man. Nor is inequality among men incompatible with the state of innocence. . . .[66]

Some of the crucial aspects of the thought of Augustine and Thomas on the relation between men and women have been outlined in order to identify the traditional elements in the position still generally affirmed in the Renaissance and Reformation period.

It would be useful to understand also the late medieval scholastic tradition of the Scotists and Occamists on this question of the nature and role of women, for Calvin normally has more in common with that tradition than with Thomas. Unfortunately there is now no study of these theologians comparable to that of Børresen on Augustine and Thomas, and to produce one would require a monograph. To generalize about that tradition on the basis of a sampling of passages is to be vulnerable to the same criticisms I made of earlier studies of Calvin: until the systematic works, the *Sentences* commentaries, have been placed together with the biblical commentaries and sermons on Genesis, the Gospels, and Paul, for example, it is not at all certain that one can have a fair estimate of this theological tradition. So I merely note here that this study of the Franciscan tradition remains on my agenda.

Though the literary world either praised or deprecated women in extreme fashion, and some commentators have accused both sorts of writers of harboring misogyny in their views, most Renaissance theologians seem to have remained fairly close to the traditional views we have sketched. They assume that both men and women are made in the image of God, but they struggle to reconcile Paul in 1 Corinthians 11 with their belief.[67] They believe women will rise at the resurrection as women, though they struggle

with a Vulgate text like Ephesians 4:13 which, by using the word
vir, man, rather than *homo,* a human being, suggests that women
would have to become perfect males. Duns Scotus seems to have
been the center of controversy on this score: some Renaissance
commentators claimed he taught that all women except the Virgin
Mary will become male in heaven, while other commentators in the
Renaissance period denied that such passages are authentically
those of Duns Scotus.[68] There remained the general conviction
that somehow by nature women are inferior to men, though there
was debate about just what the nature of their inferiority is. There
was equal insistence that by grace women might have all the
bounties of the spiritual life. Still they cannot in this world be free
of subjection to men. Maclean senses "a desire to improve the status
of woman in theology without tampering with the conceptual
structure or with the notion of her inferiority to man."[69]

It may be helpful to compare Calvin's view, as we laid out his
position, with the views of Augustine and Thomas to see where he
is merely traditional and where he takes a different turn of
thought.

How is Calvin similar to Augustine and Thomas? First, Calvin by
his very commitment to biblical authority is compelled to struggle
with the Genesis texts and the Pauline texts just as the medieval
theologians did. Calvin goes very far in recognizing the equality of
Adam and Eve in the likeness and image of God in Genesis 1, but
he then under the influence of Genesis 2 and Paul concludes that
the submission of Eve in Genesis 2 is merely a further explanation
of Genesis 1; therefore Eve was subject even in Paradise. Calvin
makes a very similar point to that of Thomas about the two kinds
of subordination. But whereas Thomas speaks merely of administrative subjection before the Fall and slavery afterward, Calvin
contrasts Eve's original mild and gentle subjection, one appropriate
to a free person, with the slavery or bondage that followed the Fall.
Calvin seems to be dealing more with a personal relationship,
whereas Thomas is dealing more abstractly with a principle of
hierarchical relationships.

Calvin agrees with the older tradition that women have equally
human souls and can receive spiritual gifts just like men. In the
spiritual realm women experience no disability. Though Calvin
does not seem to debate the issue of the nature of women's
resurrected bodies, he strongly asserts that all distinctions between
persons in heaven will be based on spiritual reward regardless of
sex or social position in this life. Like Thomas, Calvin believes it is
appropriate for women who receive the gifts of prophecy or

teaching to exercise them in private or among women rather than in the assembled community, and he does not advocate women as preachers of the Word; but Calvin admits that women have at times been called by God to use these gifts publicly.

Calvin hardly goes beyond Augustine in his assertion of the equality of the spouses in the sexual relationship, in conjugal rights to protect marital fidelity. He probably does go beyond Thomas, however. All three base their argument on Paul's teaching in 1 Corinthians 7:3–5.

So in a very general way one can say that Calvin continues the patristic and scholastic tradition of distinguishing a spiritual equality of women through the gift of the soul at creation, through grace in this life, and through the perfecting of life in the resurrection from the inequality and subordination to men that is appropriate to women in their earthly life. And he continues the patristic tradition concerning equality in conjugal rights. But as soon as one goes below that very general level, differences arise which lead us to believe that Calvin holds a fundamentally different view.

Let us look at humanist views of the biological aspects of women's nature, recalling that Calvin refers to discussion in his day of the nature of the Virgin Mary's role in the incarnation, then dismisses the medical and philosophical aspects of the debate in favor of the theological ones.[70] It is now well documented that there was indeed in the sixteenth century very considerable discussion about the physical nature of women by the doctors. The new consensus of the Renaissance physicians by 1600 was that Aristotle had been wrong in declaring the female sex inferior by nature, a defective male; the female anatomy was now considered quite normal and distinct from that of the male. But there were lingering doubts about the physical robustness of the woman and about the quality of her intellectual endowments. So the physicians as a whole remained convinced that woman's place by nature was in the home, where she could be more protected.[71] The late-sixteenth-century physicians were also generally agreed that Aristotle had been wrong in assuming that the female contributed no "seed" to the creation of a child; rather, they now followed Galen, generally believed to have taught that women as well as men contributed seminal material to the formation of a fetus. The woman was no longer seen as merely a passive nurturer biologically.[72]

Some Protestant theologians remained committed to the older view. For example, Menno Simons argues approvingly that since the woman contributes no "seed" to the child, the Virgin Mary could not contribute a sinful nature to the human Jesus. But by the same token Jesus has a mother in the same sense as any other child. If the "learned ones" were correct, however, Jesus would have been only "half a man," the sons of Moses half Midianite, and mothers would have "ten times as much right concerning the child" as the father, for the mothers carry the fetus, and nurse and care for the child long after birth. Menno argues on the basis of Scripture, not science, and he appears to be following Melchior Hoffman in this matter, though he dissociated himself from Hoffman in other ways.[73] The issue had been debated with the Reformed theologians John à Lasco and Gellius Faber in 1544 and taken up again by Faber with a pamphlet in 1552 to which Menno replied in 1554.

Therefore Calvin stands on the side of both the medical consensus and some other Reformed theologians in this debate.[74] This fact calls to mind Calvin's expression of respect for the skill of Galen, who studied exactly the wonders of the human body.[75] It is interesting that Augustine had used the absence of women's names in the biblical genealogies to argue for Aristotle's view,[76] but Calvin specifically rejects that argument. Though I have not found evidence that Calvin explicitly rejects Aristotle's view of woman as a "defective male," it certainly seems reasonable to suppose that he abandoned that along with the rest of Aristotle's female physiology. In this case the scholastic argument for the inherent incapacity of a woman to be ordained has lost an important part of its support. This allows Calvin to take up a position close to the one Thomas Aquinas rejected, that the bar to women's ordination is based on law, not inherent incapacity.[77]

Another fundamental difference between Calvin and the earlier tradition can be seen in the way he reconciles Paul and Genesis on the image of God. Augustine's exegesis finds allegorically a level within the soul itself at which one can distinguish between men and women in the degree of excellence of the image of God possessed. Thomas also identifies a "secondary sense" in which the image of God is more fully possessed by men than women. I find no evidence in Calvin of such an attempt to base male superiority on the fuller possession of the image of God. In fact, Calvin's constant repetition that any restriction on the image of God is to be limited to the "political realm" can most easily be understood as a categorical rejection of such scholastic subtlety.

Still another fundamental difference lies in the way the theologians distinguish between spiritual equality and worldly inequality of the sexes. For Augustine and Thomas any freedom or equality of women is limited to the purely spiritual experience in this life. Renouncing marriage and procreation by adopting the life of virginity permits a woman to escape subordination to men to some extent, but never completely. At least for Thomas, restrictions on women's freedom to hold public office in the church or society are rooted in divine law and biology and therefore are unchangeable. Though Calvin sees strong biblical guidance for women's subordinate role in the public life of church and society, and though he finds it appropriate for his own society that women should be subordinate, he holds on principle that the order in which women are subordinate is one determined by human law, ecclesiastical and political. Such order can legitimately be adapted to changing circumstances. God has in fact done so at times in calling women to public office, as the Scriptures demonstrate in both the Old and New Testaments. Divine law decrees unconditional equality among all human beings, an equality unequally manifest in this life. Even before the Fall woman experienced a mild subjugation to man. Since the Fall sin has so distorted all human relationships that human equality is difficult to observe. But it is present in the spiritual life, it can be increasingly manifested in the common life of Christian people, and it will be perfected at the resurrection.

One must also take into account the difference between the medieval religious worldview and that of Calvin as influenced by the Reformation rejection of the ideal of virginity. For example, Calvin, like the Scholastics, can speak of the greater freedom of a widow as compared to that of a married woman. This underlies his understanding of Paul's advice that women deacons should be widows. But celibacy for Calvin clearly depends on a special gift of God, rarely given, which has functional usefulness for a few of those who are engaged in the Lord's work but no ethical or spiritual superiority over marriage.[78]

Just as Calvin has adopted some aspects of the medieval theological tradition and transformed others to fit a new theological context, so he has also worked with the Renaissance tradition of the defense of women.[79] In comparing Calvin with the Renaissance discussions of women, his appropriations in the realm of biology have already been noted. On the whole he speaks of women with respect and dignity, though he criticizes their life-styles along with those of the men.[80] Therefore Calvin should not be classed with the Renaissance "detractors of women."

In his exegesis he reflects Renaissance concerns. He does not seem to use the arguments about Eve as the source of original sin except where the biblical text requires him to do so. Calvin finds biblical texts like the Magnificat very congenial in their emphasis on God's use of the weak to confound the mighty. Since, like sixteenth-century culture and the Renaissance doctors, he assumes that women are in some ways the weaker sex, he finds God's calls to women to rule or prophesy or teach splendid examples of evangelical teaching. In this sense he turns a somewhat negative view of women into what for him is a positive one. Evidence has been given that Calvin, like some Renaissance writers, uses Paul as an example of one who collaborated with women in God's work. Calvin balances what Paul says about women's proper subordination with what he believes Paul actually did in the life of the church, stressing that Paul was not embarrassed to admit that he had women as co-workers.

Finally, reason has been given to assume that Calvin knew that at least some Renaissance supporters of the women's cause were suggesting that women should have the right to preach; Calvin does not agree in practice, but he does not exclude that possibility in principle.

All of this suggests that when Calvin continues through all the editions of the *Institutes* to teach that women's silence in the church, a symbol of women's inability to hold church office, is a matter of humanly decreed order in the church, subject to changing circumstances, he is surely not being careless or even confused, but rather *very* cautiously intentional. Calvin appears to have been helped by the *querelle des femmes,* as well as by the Renaissance study of history (discussed in chapter 2), to reevaluate traditional teaching of women's subordination in the public arena and to conclude that it is historically conditioned and therefore subject to change.

On the other hand, Calvin seems to have found the more radical proponents of the women's cause, like Agrippa, who advocated practical change, to be threatening to the piety of the church.

5

Women's Freedom
in Church Order:
Calvin in
the Reformation Context

Having explored Calvin's own views of women's freedom in church order and placed them in the medieval and Renaissance context, we now must turn to the Reformation context. It will be helpful to compare Calvin's exegesis of some key biblical texts with that of Luther, to point out some similarities with Bucer, Calvin's colleague during his years in Strasbourg, and to contrast Calvin's view of "indifferent things" in church order with that of a variety of sixteenth-century Protestant confessions. This exploration will assist in clarifying where Calvin is unique and where he merely echoes the thought of other Reformers.

But it will also be important to examine the available evidence of how Protestant women themselves who had some contact with Calvin understood their freedom in church order. Such an investigation may well help us in understanding Calvin's particular concerns and sensitivities.

The last chapter showed that the Renaissance writers often based their higher views of women's status on differing biological, philosophical, and pedagogical evaluations of the nature of women. They have then sometimes reinterpreted biblical passages in a way which would support their views. But they also had new exegetical skills with which to understand the biblical text itself.

To what extent could one make the same judgment of the Reformers? The process in their case would seem to be one step more complex. Leaders of the mainstream of the Reformation were themselves deeply influenced by the changed intellectual climate; and Calvin is among those most deeply touched by Renaissance thought. He knew the questions being raised about women's proper role and fundamental nature; he had personal contact with learned women of the Renaissance and thus firsthand experience of the effectiveness of pedagogical theory about women's intellectual capacity to appropriate humanistic education; and he had acquired the intellectual, historical, and philological tools with which to renew biblical exegesis. We saw, for example, his appropriation of the Renaissance notion of "accommodation" and its usefulness in historical study of biblical materials. He was better able to place biblical passages in their particular historical context than earlier exegetes had been.

The priesthood of all believers. Like all the Reformers, Calvin seems to have also approached the question of women's proper role and freedom from the context of the doctrine of the priesthood of all believers. This doctrine was surely proclaimed by Luther in the context of Christian freedom. Men and women alike experienced a new sense of freedom from control by a clerical hierarchy and a new sense of dignity of the lay person. The doctrine of Christian vocation elevated the religious status of the housewife as well as the cobbler. But in many ways the new freedom was experienced less fully by women than by men.

One consequence of the doctrine of the priesthood of all believers was a new stress on popular education for most Protestants. Reformation teaching of the "priesthood of all believers" made it very important that all Christians should be capable of reading the Bible and other religious literature. Church-related schools for both boys and girls had existed in Geneva prior to the Reformation. Public schooling was added as early as 1428 for boys—but not girls—in Geneva,[1] part of a general improvement in education of the laity in the later Middle Ages. But the Reformation provided the impetus to expand and develop these small beginnings.

As early as 1524 Luther called on the civil authorities to establish schools to educate the children.[2] After 1536, the official beginning of the Reformation in Geneva, all Genevan children were required to attend school. Those families that could pay for tuition were expected to do so, but the schoolmaster was to be paid by the city so that he could feed and teach the poor children without fees.[3] Girls and boys learned reading, arithmetic, catechism, and writing. At least after 1541, girls seem to have had their own public school for primary instruction, but there were complaints for many years that no public secondary school for girls existed in the city.[4]

Joyce Irwin notes that the Anabaptist movement was far more suspicious of education, both for men and women. She wonders whether the almost anti-intellectual mind-set of this tradition and the consequent lack of educational opportunity may not be a significant factor in women's failure to profit more from the "anti-hierarchical biases of their sects. . . . In spite of democratic tendencies, the women remained entirely subordinate to the men, both in the home and in the church."[5]

One must be very careful not to suggest that increased education in the sixteenth century would necessarily work against the theological tradition of subordination of women, even in a setting where there were more democratic tendencies. Nevertheless, even modest gains in basic literacy for women certainly did open the way to some measure of increased freedom for women in church and society. And we will see numerous examples of unusually well educated women who played decidedly nontraditional roles in the church.

The priesthood of all believers is also related to the general Protestant stress on the dignity of marriage as the normal life for all the saints. Protestant rejection of the ethical superiority of the counsels of perfection in favor of a single ethic for all Christians removed the basic argument for clerical celibacy. Celibacy can be justified, in Calvin's view, as a use of God-given liberty for special cases where greater freedom from family responsibilities may be useful for a particular form of service. But this celibacy related to mission is not superior to marriage.[6]

Many writers of the Reformation period experienced this new view of marriage as a liberation from papal laws that they believed were inhuman and contrary to God's original intent in creation, a liberation from conflict between religious obedience and the good gifts of God in creation, a liberation that benefited both men and women.[7] It was also perceived as a liberation of communities from various problems created by large numbers of clerics who could not in fact remain celibate. Strasbourg, for example, was enraged in 1519 and 1520 by a series of attacks by clerics on women that led the burghers to believe the unmarried clerics threatened the safety of the women of the city and public order.[8] There is also ample evidence that at the time of the Reformation the pastoral relation of women to unmarried confessors was perceived to be a threat to women's chastity.[9] Concerns were also growing about church exploitation of these problems. Katherine Zell, wife of the first Reformed minister to marry in Strasbourg, in her published tract in defense of clerical marriage, was one of many to complain about cradle taxes, collected by the bishops when children were born to their priests, as a form of financial exploitation.[10]

Apart from these ways in which the new view of marriage resulted in some greater freedom for men and women, Protestant marriage gave women very little more freedom than married women had had before. The Reformers generally see patriarchal marriage as a God-given blessing that needs only to be humanized by greater love and respect. Women are free to teach their children and manage their households, tasks that are seen as offering ample opportunity for the use of their managerial skills; but they must remain subject to their husbands as head of the household. Even physical abuse by a husband must be borne patiently unless there is genuine danger of serious injury or renunciation of faith.[11]

It does seem to be true, however, that Calvin and Bucer place more stress on mutuality in marriage than others.[12] Calvin speaks of the authority of the husband in marriage more as "that of a society than of a kingdom."[13] His commentary on Genesis 1 and 2 stresses the companionship of Adam and Eve. Both Bucer and Calvin are unusual in the sixteenth century in permitting women equal access to divorce in the case where they have been wronged by adultery and in permitting the innocent partner in adultery to remarry.[14] It is important to realize, however, that few divorces were actually granted in Calvin's Geneva.[15]

When one considers the traditional list of the purposes of marriage: procreation, avoidance of fornication, and mutual assistance and love, it is also in Bucer and the Reformed tradition that one can first observe significant change. Whereas traditionally procreation is seen as the first end of marriage, Bucer says, "The true and entire purpose of marriage is that the spouses serve one another in all love and fidelity, that the woman be the aid and the flesh of the man and the man the head and savior of the woman."[16] The Second Helvetic Confession of 1566 in the section on marriage makes no mention of procreation as the purpose of marriage and mentions the remedy of incontinence only parenthetically. God wishes man and woman to cleave inseparably to each other and to live in one highest love and concord.[17] The Westminster Confession in the following century would also list the mutual help of husband and wife as the first purpose of marriage.[18] This shifting of priority in marriage away from procreation or prevention of sin to the mutual cherishing of husband and wife and their help to one another does represent significant change in the understanding of marriage.

Mention should also be made of the revival of the role of the pastor's wife by Protestantism after several centuries when this role did not legally or officially exist in the West, though concubinage certainly did. The pastor's wife has been called the "pilot model of the new woman" created by Reformation influence.[19] Not all of these wives limited their activities to the household. Katherine Zell's published defense of clerical marriage in Strasbourg has been mentioned. She also wrote letters of protest of various sorts to officials of church and state; she published a treatise of consolation for a city magistrate who was ill, and four pamphlets of hymns written by others, to which she added a preface. She helped nurse a nephew in the hospital and then made strong recommendations to the city council for improving deplorable conditions there. Just before her death she defiantly conducted an unauthorized funeral service for a dead Schwenckfeldian woman whose husband was not willing to let the pastor announce her apostasy from the true faith.[20] Such activity demonstrates that spirited women with a vision of the priesthood of all believers often changed roles by assuming freedom that was never officially granted to them.

The priesthood of all believers also gave some women new freedom to participate in public worship. The medieval church did not permit women to take part in liturgical singing. There was some initial reluctance even among Protestants to permit women such a role. Johann Eberlin von Günzburg in his 1521 proposals for ideal reform still specified that "nuns and other women" should not sing or read publicly in church.[21] But within a very few years Strasbourg and Wittenberg had encouraged virtually all the Protestant churches to institute congregational singing. The Swiss churches under Zwingli's influence were an exception.[22] But since Geneva was reformed by leaders much influenced by Zwingli, Geneva in the earliest years of the Reformation had no congregational singing. Calvin after his return from exile in Strasbourg succeeded in beginning the singing of the Psalms by the whole congregation, believing this to be the practice of the early church and a heartwarming part of worship.[23]

But Roman Catholics still considered this participation by women most inappropriate. A Catholic in Paris describes the Reformed worship as

> without law, without order, without harmony. . . . The minister begins. Everybody follows—men, women, children, servants, chambermaids. . . . No one is on the same verse. . . . The fine-voiced maidens let loose their hums and trills . . . so the young men will be sure to listen. How wrong of Calvin to let women sing in church.[24]

Calvin acknowledges that his Roman opponents ridicule the Genevan practice of having the women as well as the men sing the

Psalms together in public worship, and in the vernacular as well, but he believes the women should fully participate in this way.

> If only the Holy Spirit bears testimony to us from heaven, while he repudiates the confused, unmeaning sounds which are uttered elsewhere, we are content.[25]

Women's public leadership in the church. Except for Calvin, the mainstream Reformers seem to be unanimous that public leadership in worship or preaching is forbidden to women by God. And we have seen that Calvin is ambivalent on this question. On the one hand, he knows of biblical women prophets; but on the other hand he expresses some puzzlement as to how, for example, the daughters of Philip had exercised their prophetic gifts in the early church without scandalizing the community. He thought they might have prophesied privately. He clearly argues in both the *Institutes* and some commentaries that the injunction for women to be silent in church is in the realm of human law and could be adapted to changing cultures and needs of the church. On the other hand, he just as clearly communicates his conviction that the sight of a woman preaching in church with her head uncovered would be scandalous. It is uncertain to what extent it is the preaching and to what extent it is the uncovered head that is offensive. He also at times argues that it is improper for a woman who ought to be subject to men to exercise authority over them by preaching and teaching. So the priesthood of all believers did not for Calvin automatically free the church to call its women members to public leadership in the congregation.

Luther's commentary on 1 Timothy will give us a helpful point of comparison with Calvin. When Luther deals with 1 Timothy 2:11–14, where Paul tells women to learn in silence with submissiveness, he asks fewer questions about the way to interpret this passage than Calvin. He does show some awareness that women are treated differently in different cultures and asserts briefly that Paul was speaking against the Greek women, who have always been more "ingenious and clever" than others. And he mentions the problem that there have been apparent exceptions to this rule, biblical women skilled at management and with authority: Huldah, Deborah, Jael, the wise woman of Abel (2 Sam. 20:14–21), Philip's daughters, Queen Candace of Ethiopia (Acts 8:27). Luther dismisses the whole problem by saying that Paul is concerned that men be in authority when men are present, and that Huldah, Deborah, the woman of Abel, and the daughters of Philip are exceptional cases because they were unmarried. Since 1 Timothy

2:12 really means that wives should have no authority over their husbands, the problem is resolved, Luther thinks. Since Huldah and Deborah had no husbands, they did not rule over husbands. It is not clear why Jael, the wife of Heber (Judg. 4:17), is brought in here by Luther, except perhaps simply as a clever manager. And it is certainly unclear why other unmarried women could not have authority over the community, since at the outset Luther explains that this passage is dealing with public matters, ministry in the public assembly of the church. Nonetheless Luther understands Paul to be protecting the biblical order that man must be the head of the woman, since Adam was created first, and that women are not permitted to speak in the assembly when men are present. For a woman to challenge a man's teaching would create disorder. "By divine and human law . . . Adam is the master of the woman."[26] Still, at the end of the chapter Luther mystifies us further by adding, "If the Lord were to raise up a woman in order for us to listen to her, we would allow her to rule like Huldah."[27] Then he moves on to the next section of the text.

In general we can observe that Luther seems much less aware of problems raised by the 1 Timothy passage than Calvin. The traditional cases of exceptional biblical women are cited, but the only explanation offered is their unmarried state. There is none of Calvin's preoccupation with the freedom of the Spirit to break through the normal order of creation. Luther simply accepts Paul's argument for male priority by Adam's creation before Eve in time as appropriate in divine, if not always in human, affairs, whereas Calvin finds that argument very weak, perhaps because of Renaissance criticisms of it. We also notice that Luther seems to be propounding an interpretation of Paul's second argument very similar to the one Calvin flatly rejects: Adam really was not deceived by the serpent; he just wanted to please his wife. He did not go astray himself but was deceived by Eve, the real cause of transgression.[28] Finally, we notice that in 1 Timothy 2:15, the verse promising women salvation through bearing children if they continue in faith, there is a more direct focus on childbearing as punishment and as salutary than in Calvin. Luther has no admonitions here to husbands about their obligations in marriage and parenthood parallel to those of Calvin in his sermon.

Chapter 3 above discussed Calvin's explanations in both the *Institutes* and the commentaries about the public ministry of women as deacons in the early church. Was this a general Reformation point of view? Apparently not, since Luther seems unaware of it.

Commenting on Paul's discussion in 1 Timothy 5:3–16 concerning the widows, Calvin understands the first part of the passage to refer to the widows more generally, the second part concerning the enrollment of widows to refer to those who were ordained to public ministry and took a vow of celibacy to keep them free for ministry. But Luther takes the second section as a discussion of widows merely supported charitably by the church and feels that widows younger than sixty should be able to care for themselves and not become burdens on the church. So he puzzles considerably over the reason for insisting that the widows accepted have been married only once, and he is even more puzzled over the meaning of the pledge violated if they should again marry.[29] Nowhere does he propose Calvin's solution to this problem.

It seems likely that Calvin got his idea of the women deacons from Bucer in Strasbourg, on whom he is often dependent in matters of church order. Bucer had proposed in 1532 that a diaconate of both men and women be included among the ministers of the church. But the ecclesiastical ordinances passed in 1534 excluded the diaconate altogether, and a later attempt by Bucer to include it also failed.[30]

One also can find the idea of women deacons in a work entitled *Treatise on Christian Discipline and Governance,* published in 1562 by Jean Morély, a lay member of the French Reformed Church who also resided for some time in Geneva. Morély sent this treatise to Calvin for his evaluation.[31] Morély's proposal of women deacons is included in a general discussion of the four ministries of the church: pastors, elders, deacons, and teachers, a structure of ministry advocated by both Bucer and Calvin. This treatise on the whole demonstrates a very strong concern to reform the church in more democratic ways, and it set off quite a storm of controversy in France and Geneva that precluded any immediate implementation of the proposal for women deacons.[32] For example, Morély stresses the importance for the liberty of the church of electing elders from the whole community to avoid oligarchy and to be sure the church really chooses its governing council rather than merely being subject to it.[33]

Morély believes that in the early church there was a small group of principal deacons with an important spiritual ministry who also received the alms and supervised the care of the poor and needy. But for the actual ministry to the poor a special election was held, and the persons chosen for the task took vows. This group included doctors and surgeons and others who were called deacons in the sense of the etymology of the word, but they were under the supervision of the principal deacons. Deaconesses were also part of the latter group.[34]

Because of the great number offering themselves, Paul and the church could choose the most virtuous and those least distracted by other responsibilities. Therefore Paul sets down the requirements that a widow should be at least sixty, have been the wife of one husband and have raised her children. But Morély insists that these restrictions are not necessary for all times; he believes the early community also used married women in this role. Women seem to be the most proper sex for caring for the sick; and the age above sixty served to be sure the women were above suspicion. Unlike the "lazy" orders of nuns, the office of deaconesses should be one of daily service and action, not of "parade." It would be good for such an office to be restored.[35]

Robert Kingdon notes that Morély acknowledges in general his debt to Calvin as well as Bucer, and that he argues regularly from the authority of Scripture.[36] But Kingdon seems nonetheless surprised by Morély's argument that Paul's rules for the deaconesses are not rules for all time. Kingdon takes this as evidence that "while he normally insisted that Scripture was the 'Word of God,' and should be accepted without demur, he was not completely consistent and invariable in this rule."[37]

Morély's argument could perhaps at first glance be understood to be completely consistent with Calvin's own principles for the understanding of church order in relation to Scripture. At the beginning of Morély's discussion of the ecclesiastical offices of elder and deacon, for example, he points out that these are part of the external governance *(police)* and constitution of the church, necessary for order and to avoid confusion.[38] The advice of Paul concerning widows in the service of the church would seem to be a clear parallel to the advice of Paul concerning silence and veiling, advice that Calvin also claimed was related to order and decorum of the church and could be adapted to changing needs and circumstances.

But the preface to the treatise, addressed to Pierre Viret by Morély, suggests that Morély has either not understood or has intentionally rejected Calvin's view of the church's freedom in matters of external order. Morély believes that God once ordained his chosen form of church government at the time of ancient Israel. Since it was distorted through the centuries, it was re-instituted in the early church by Jesus Christ, king and legislator, and the apostles. But God does not want to change this perfect form of government, which Morély lays out.

That person seems to me to be greatly mistaken who believes that this government and order of the church of the Lord is an indifferent thing and that it ought to change at every instant, as persons and other circumstances of place and time change. For if the ways and counsels of the Lord are also different from ours, that is the distance of the heavens from the earth; also it is necessary for us to confess that there is no order better, nor more certain, nor more honorable, nor more to our contentment, nor more necessary to the church of the Lord than that one which he once established.[39]

Morély feels that there will be problems for the unity of the church if a variety of constitutions and orders appears. Any other orders that have been instituted are extraordinary and a concession to weakness; they should be replaced by the one revealed in Scripture. The laws of the Lord Jesus, our eternal king and unique legislator, are eternal and belong to all ages.[40]

It appears, therefore, that Morély has been influenced by Bucer and Calvin in his view that Scripture teaches a fourfold ministry of pastors, elders, deacons, and doctors, and by Calvin and possibly Bucer in his view that there were two sorts of deacons and that the widows of 1 Timothy 5:9 are deaconesses. But given his different understanding of church order as law given by Christ for all ages, his argument for flexibility about Paul's rules is not likely to be that of Calvin. Rather, he seems to suggest that there are other examples in the New Testament of married women serving as deaconesses which relativize Paul's particular rules.[41]

It is interesting that Morély, for all his general concern about the freedom of the church, the rights of the whole church to choose its ministers, and the equality of all received at the Lord's Table, nonetheless specifies that in organizing disciplinary assemblies of all the members of a congregation, women should be excluded because Paul forbids them to speak in the assembly. Children under fifteen and merchants who speculate in necessary commodities are also to be excluded.[42] Even as radical a "democratic" Reformer as Morély was not prepared to give women full freedom in the church. His reading of the Scriptures would not permit it.

We have seen that others read the Scriptures differently. Agrippa of Nettesheim points to the prophecy of Joel 2 about the pouring out of the Spirit on women as justification for women's freedom to preach and teach. Katherine Zell, whom Calvin surely knew during his years in Strasbourg,[43] in her public defense of clerical marriage responds to criticisms of her feistiness by quoting Joel also:

You remind me that the apostle Paul told women to be silent in church. I would remind you of the word of this same apostle that in Christ there is no longer male nor female and of the prophecy of Joel: "I will pour forth my spirit upon all flesh and your sons and your *daughters* will prophesy." I do not pretend to be John the Baptist rebuking the Pharisees. I do not claim to be Nathan upbraiding David. I aspire only to be Balaam's ass, castigating his master.[44]

Luther seems very comfortable with the Joel text. He treats it briefly and straightforwardly as dealing with the kingdom inaugurated at Pentecost and the public revelation of the Holy Spirit. In this new kingdom "there will be no distinction of persons. . . . Without difference sons and daughters will prophesy and teach."[45] Present distinctions between maidservants and menservants will cease.

This is a very obvious passage against that ghostly papist priesthood in which they do not want just anyone to be priests but where there is a respect of persons. Christ says, however, that all his faithful people are going to be priests. After all, what else does a priesthood require except the declaration of the works of and Word of God? No one can deny that here this is being granted to all Christians. . . .[46]

For Luther this passage speaks clearly to the priesthood of all believers without apparently threatening in any way Luther's assumption that only men will be pastors.

What then does Calvin do with the Joel prophecy? Calvin sees in the promise of the pouring out of the Spirit on all flesh that after the advent of Jesus Christ, in the "new restitution of the church," the Spirit will be much more abundant than ever before. Whereas in Israel the gift of prophecy was a rare gift, given to few, in the new church it will be abundant. Therefore he thinks the prophet is engaging in hyperbole to make this point. One should understand that the exuberance of the prophet in extolling the grace of God is to be taken into account. For Paul says that not all are called to be prophets, though Peter claims that the prophecy has been fulfilled in the pouring out of the Spirit on the church. So Joel is not promising that all will be called to the office of teaching. Rather, Joel foretells what was experienced by the early church: Christians had such light of teaching that they could be compared with prophets; in general the most contemptible of the Christians were peers in understanding with the old prophets. Calvin notes that women are included in this outpouring of Spirit, and he acknowledges that there were prophetesses under the law. But he does not here discuss at all the question of women holding public office. He merely notes that the gift of the Spirit and the call to the teaching office are not to be equated.[47] Calvin's comments on the Joel prophecy quoted in Acts 2:17 are not essentially different. Here, too, the emphasis is on prophecy as the gift of rare understanding open to all believers under the gospel.[48]

Calvin's greater caution in dealing with the prophecy of Joel may be related to the fact that a number of Reformed women in France were behaving as though Joel should be interpreted in its more obvious sense—as Agrippa had suggested. Natalie Davis describes their activities:

> Some of the women prisoners in the French jails preached to "the great consolation" of both male and female listeners. Our ex-Calvinist jurist Florimond de Raemond gave several examples, both from the Protestant conventicles and from the regular Reformed services as late as 1572, of women who while waiting for a preacher to arrive had gone up to pulpits and read from the Bible. One *théologienne* even took public issue with her pastor. Finally, in some of the Reformed Churches southwest of Paris—in areas where weavers and women had been early converts—a movement started to permit lay persons to prophesy. This would have allowed both women and unlearned men to get up in church and speak on holy things.[49]

The Reformed churches were experiencing tension between, on the one hand, the new teaching of the priesthood of all believers and the freedom of Christians in the Spirit, and, on the other, Paul's injunctions for women to be silent in church and traditional restrictions on lay leadership in public worship. Women were hearing the gospel differently than the male theologians.

This same tension was experienced in the early years of the Reformation in other contexts as well. There is evidence that women gained greater freedom temporarily in a variety of Protestant movements, only to lose it in time as new institutions were firmly established. Calvin Pater notes evidence that women were prophesying along with lay men in the early years of Karlstadt's movement.[50] And Roland Bainton's books on women in the Reformation call attention to many untraditional roles that women played in widely scattered areas of the Reformation.[51] We will see evidence of the same phenomenon in Geneva.

Women as political rulers. If women's subordination was so generally taught by the theologians as proper in marriage and in the church, did it also extend to political office? If women were not to rule over men in the church, how could they be legitimate queens? A very considerable amount of printer's ink was spilled in the sixteenth-century debate about gynecocracy, or the rule of women. John Neale has commented that for many statesmen of this period, government was "a mystery revealed only to men. They had less faith in Deborah than John Knox, and were more dangerous for being more reasonable."[52] But theologians and literary people also joined the discussion. In the writings of Juan Vives, Sir David Lyndsay, Laurence Humphrey, Jean Bodin, George Buchanan, Edmund Spenser, Christopher Goodman, and others, one can find the traditional arguments against the rule of women. On the other hand, Agrippa of Nettesheim's treatise on women and Thomas Elyot's *The Defence of Good Women* (1540) argued in favor of women's capacity to rule successfully.[53]

At the center of this furor in mid-century was the Scottish Reformer John Knox, who had worked with Calvin in Geneva for a time among the English-speaking refugees. In his treatise *The First Blast of the Trumpet Against the Monstrous Regiment of Women*, published in Geneva in 1558, he announced that he could see nothing but evil in the fact that women, contrary to nature and Scripture, as he believed, were usurping men's authority in his day by ruling nations.[54] Though God has occasionally raised up re- markable women to commanding positions, women by nature are "weake, fraile, impacient, feble, and foolishe; and experience hath declared them to be unconstant, variable, cruell, and lacking the spirit of counsel and regiment."[55] Even without the help of Scripture, Aristotle rightly understood that even a man too much dominated by his wife is a poor ruler.[56] Eve's malediction after the Fall to be subject to her husband's will (Gen. 3:16) and the New Testament injunctions to silence in the congregation (1 Tim. 2:9–15 and 1 Cor. 14:34–35), together with the Fathers' writings in the same tone, gave Knox confidence that Mary, "Jesabel of England," would soon be put down from her tyranny by God.[57] And in fact she died a few months later.

Knox's attack had been directed at Mary Tudor, a Roman Catholic queen. Knox had also had unpleasant experiences with other Catholic women rulers: Mary of Lorraine and Mary Stuart. Richard Greaves argues that Knox's hostility to them is related to his hostility to the Virgin Mary as understood in Catholicism.[58] Even without psychology one can grasp the problem for Knox of Catholic rulers. But at the death of Mary Tudor, Knox found himself confronted by still another woman ruler. This time it was Elizabeth of England, a Protestant, who became head of the English church and was understandably also offended by Knox's *Blast*. It could certainly suggest to her subjects that they should not obey her. Though Knox made some clumsy attempts at conciliating Elizabeth, he seems to have retained his conscientious objections to female rulers till his death.[59]

Calvin, because of his close associations with Knox, was caught in the crossfire of this engagement. In fact Knox had consulted both Calvin and Bullinger on the issue of women's ruling some time before publishing his treatise, so he was well aware that they did not really share his views.[60] But when Elizabeth was rather cool about the revised commentary on Isaiah dedicated to her by Calvin, Calvin felt obliged to write Sir William Cecil, Elizabeth's secretary, in 1559 to distance himself from Knox's work and make his own position clear.[61]

Calvin's own view expressed to Bullinger in 1544, before the debate became very public, is that though women's rule differs from the legitimate order of nature and is to be considered a punishment from God, it should be patiently tolerated. God has at times, for example with Deborah, raised up women of heroic spirit and given them extraordinary grace. Though such a situation may appear to be "mere confusion," one should accept it and pray for a spirit of moderation and prudence. He expresses essential agreement with the position of Bullinger and Zurich, which explicitly recognizes the need to receive a woman ruler if she accedes according to the law of the land.[62] Calvin's statement is brief, calm, and, compared with that of Knox, noticeably lacking in invective, as is Bullinger's. Essentially the same points are made in the letter to Cecil after Knox's *Blast* created so much controversy. Calvin does, however, add a reference to Isaiah's prophecy that wicked Israel will receive women rulers (Isa. 3:12), in which he distinguishes the prerogatives of queens as "nourishers of the church" *(ecclesiae nutrices)* from those of private women. He concludes that it would not be proper to overturn legitimate women rulers ordained by the peculiar providence of God, in view of longstanding custom and public consent.[63]

We saw earlier Calvin's apparent uneasiness with the Joel prophecy, perhaps because of the way it was being used to support women's leadership in the church. But in the context of women's political leadership, Calvin seems to find no difficulty using the Isaiah prophecy in a supportive way, though it, too, has some polemical history in the sixteenth century. Argula von Grumbach, a Bavarian noblewoman, in 1523 wrote a vigorous letter of protest to the faculty of the University of Ingolstadt about their treatment of a young Lutheran faculty member. In defense of her intervention she says:

I am not unacquainted with the word of Paul that women should be silent in church . . . but, when no man will or can speak, I am driven by the word of the Lord when he said, "He who confesses me on earth, him will I confess and he who denies me, him will I deny," . . . and I take comfort in the words of the prophet Isaiah . . . , "I will send you children to be your princes and women to be your rulers." . . . I send you not a woman's ranting, but the Word of God. I write as a member of the church of Christ against which the gates of hell shall not prevail.[64]

Calvin's attitude of hopefulness about the accession of Elizabeth to the throne of England seems quite consistent with his accepting attitude toward the many French noblewomen with whom he corresponded over the years, especially Marguerite and Jeanne d'Albret, queens of Navarre, and Renée de France, all rulers of lands. He hoped in vain for Marguerite's and Renée's open confession of Protestantism; but he assisted Renée and Marguerite's Reformed daughter, Jeanne, in reforming their religion and their lands by sending ministers to work with them.[65]

In fact French noblewomen played a significant political role in the Reformation, and Calvin recognized his need of their support if new territories were to be opened to evangelical faith.[66] Jeanne d'Albret also appeared in the ecclesiastical context of the national Synod of La Rochelle of 1571.[67] Renée's role of patronage with respect to Reformed congregations was so active that her Calvinist pastor, François de Morel, became uncomfortable and complained to Calvin. He feared the Calvinist consistories would be ridiculed by Catholics and Anabaptists for allowing women to rule them.[68] Dutch Calvinist noblewomen also took a leading role in the Reformation.[69]

It appears then that Calvin's attitude toward women rulers has been particularly shaped by his French experience and is considerably more positive than that of Knox. Calvin also seems to be more open than Luther. This contrast should perhaps be seen in the context of Chrisman's judgment that French culture was far more supportive of a public life for women than German culture in the sixteenth century, even though Bainton provides counterexamples.[70] Whereas Calvin seems conscious that the issue is under debate, Luther does not.

Luther explains his attitude very clearly in comments on Ecclesiastes 7:28 in 1532. He insists that the female sex, as creature of God, should not be damned, and that the sex is to be distinguished from its vices. But the sexes have different vocations given by God and should be faithful to them. Women are created to nourish and educate children, and they handle children much better than men are able to do. Women should do their task virtuously and piously and be subject to their husbands. It is men who have been created to rule. Luther knows the stories of the Amazons, but he believes them to be fables. He takes more seriously the historical accounts of Ethiopian queens, but believes the Ethiopian custom is foolish. Luther sees no divine permission for women to rule at all, though he concedes that it may be possible for a woman to serve in the place of a king if she has a senate of male princes by whose counsel all things are administered.[71]

The Genevan context. So far we have tended to look at Calvin more in the context of his French background and over against his reforming colleagues elsewhere than in the context of Geneva, where so much of his reforming work was done. What can we learn about the freedom of women in the Genevan Reformation before Calvin's arrival?

We are very fortunate to have at our disposal the chronicle of a nun of the Order of St. Claire, Jeanne de Jussie, who was living in a convent in Geneva during the years just before the Reformation, when Protestant adherents were increasing. A young nun who had learned to write in a Geneva school before entering the convent,[72] she chronicles the events of the years 1526 to 1535 in her volume *The Leaven of Calvinism; or, The Beginning of the Heresy of Geneva.* It is a spirited account, if not a very elegant one in style, with far more references to women than one is accustomed to find in sixteenth-century documents! Sister Jeanne ends her work with the sisters filing out of the city of Geneva, which they now found so hostile to their vocation, and reestablishing themselves at Annecy in France, where she eventually became the abbess.[73]

Sister Jeanne has the strong conviction that the women were more loyal to the Catholic faith than the men.[74] Though many monks and priests disgracefully married, she reports, only one of all the sisters of St. Claire was perverted, and she had not come with good intentions. The others were all strongly persuaded of the heresy of the new faith.[75] There were often torn loyalties in divided families, but Sister Jeanne tells enthusiastically of the firmness in faith of many "good Catholic women" whose husbands were heretics. There was the woman who suddenly died of sadness when her husband had the new baby baptized by the Protestant pastor, Farel.[76] Many others were "more than martyrs," beaten and tormented for their unwillingness to desert the true faith. Three, locked in a room because they would not attend the Protestant

Easter Communion, escaped by a window to attend Mass.[77] Two "notable bourgeois Catholic women" came, in 1535, to the convent at some risk to console the sisters when Protestant men were ransacking it, destroying pieces of art, and trying to persuade the nuns to give up their vocation.[78]

On Good Friday of 1533 the population of the city was lining up in two armed camps. The Catholics were eager to root out the "infection" that was troubling the city.[79]

> The wives of the Christians assembled, saying that if it happens that our husbands fight against those infidels, let us also make war and kill their heretic wives, so that the race may be exterminated. In this assembly of women there were a good seven hundred children of twelve to fifteen years, firmly decided to do a good deed with their mothers: the women carried stones in their laps, and most of the children carried little rapiers . . . , others stones in their breast, hat and bonnet.[80]

The same day, after a Catholic man had been fatally wounded by a blow on the head, the "Christian women" let out a great cry and turned on the wife of a Lutheran, shouting, "As the beginning of our war, let's throw this bitch in the Rhone!" She escaped into a house, but the women in their anger threw everything in the shop on the ground. Meanwhile the nuns of St. Claire in tears and great devotion prayed for the victory of the Christians and the return of the erring to the path of salvation. Some "good Christian women" came to warn the sisters that if the heretics won, they planned to force all the sisters, young and old, to marry. But the day passed without bloodshed,[81] and a truce was eventually arranged.

The Protestant women are never portrayed as violent. Nonetheless by 1534 two sorts of aggravation are attributed to them: they ostentatiously work on feast days, and they try to persuade the nuns to leave the convent.

While the Catholics were in festival procession in the streets, the Lutheran women sat in their windows for everyone to see them spinning and doing needlework. There were reprisals. After some of them did laundry on the day after Easter and Pentecost, their clothing was thrown in the Rhone. A big Lutheran woman was hit in the head with the distaff someone had snatched from her, then she was trampled in the mud.[82]

As early as 1534 a Lutheran woman, a relative of one of the nuns, came to visit the convent and used the opportunity to pour out her "venom" on the "poor nuns." She claimed that the world had been in error and idolatry till now, that the commandments of

God had not been truly taught, that their predecessors had lived wrongly, and finally added "detestable words" on the Sacrament. When the nuns did not succeed in quieting her by their objections, they finally barred the door in her face while she continued to talk.[83]

Twice when city officials came with Protestants to ascertain whether the nuns were being constrained in any way to remain in the convent against their will, they brought Protestant women with them. One, Marie Dentière, of Picardy, had been an abbess, but now was married and "meddled with preaching, and perverting people of devotion." In spite of the nuns' scorn for her defection, she persevered in her attempt to persuade them to her new view. Sister Jeanne reports that she said:

> O poor creatures! If only you knew that it is good to be with a handsome husband, and how agreeable it is to God. I lived for a long time in that darkness and hypocrisy where you are, but God alone made me understand the abuse of my pitiful life, and I came to the true light of truth.[84]

Regretting her life in "mental corruption and idleness," she took five hundred ducats from the abbey treasury and left that "unhappiness." "Thanks to God alone, I already have five handsome children, and I live salutarily."[85] The sisters replied by spitting on her in detestation.

Another time Madame Claude, wife of Levet, an apothecary, was brought to the sisters, for she also "meddled in preaching." When the Protestants asked "that diabolical tongue" to "do her duty," she began to preach, disparaging the Virgin Mary, the saints, and the state of virginity, praising marriage, and claiming that all the apostles had been married, quoting Paul's approval of being two in one flesh, and "perverting Holy Scripture." When the nuns vigorously protested and asked her to be taken away, they were told by the Protestant men that she was a holy creature, illuminated by God, who had won many souls to the truth by her holy preaching and divine teaching.[86]

It is interesting that "Lutheranism" for Sister Jeanne is primarily identified with contempt for the Sacrament, iconoclasm, and this new lauding of marriage. A new form of marriage service is reported in 1534 as performed by Farel, consisting in no solemnity of devotion but "only their commandment to join together and multiply the world," and "some dissolute words that I do not write at all for it is shameful to a chaste heart to think them."[87]

Apart from the "false" sister who became Protestant and married, publicly maligning the sisters' way of life, they believed, only one nun emerges from the journal as a personality. That is the Mother Vicar, who first assists the frail and elderly abbess in dealing with the Protestants and city officials who come to disturb the nuns' way of life and then is asked by the nuns to take charge of them.[88] When ordered to attend a public disputation on religion, she and the abbess decline respectfully on the grounds that they have vowed to live the cloistered life. Furthermore, "it is not the task of women to dispute, it is not ordained for women . . . , since it is forbidden to uneducated people to meddle in interpreting Holy Scripture, and a woman has never been called to dispute or witness."[89] But she proves to be a very aggressive and vocal advocate of her own way of life, brashly telling off the Protestant men with as much irreverence as they show her. When she was asked why the nuns wear such garments, she replied that they like them, then in turn asked the questioner why he was dressed so pompously.[90] When Farel and Viret came to preach to the nuns, she put up such a racket of protest that she was removed from the room. But she continued to beat on the wall and cry warnings to the sisters not to listen, telling the preacher he was wasting his effort, till Farel forgot what he was talking about.[91] After this experience he decided not to return to preach there again.[92]

Our glance at the Reformation as seen by Sister Jeanne gives evidence that Protestant teaching in praise of marriage seemed to unsympathetic contemporaries to be of considerable importance in the new faith and a radical departure from the tradition. We also see that though the Protestants talked of "freedom" to the nuns they were perceived as bringing a new form of constraint, a constraint to marry and be subject to husbands. Furthermore, Sister Jeanne's journal helps to confirm our impression that women played a more active role in bringing about the Reformation—and opposing it—than has usually been assumed.

Certain aspects of Sister Jeanne's chronicle are supported by a chronicle written in Geneva by a Protestant pastor, Anthoine Fromment, beginning in 1532. Fromment agrees that women at first were very resistant to the Reformation.[93] There were none at all in the first group gathered around Farel and Sonnier. In fact, Fromment says he was very nearly thrown into the Rhone River by a group of women stirred up by the priests.[94]

But Claudine Levet, described as an honest citizen of Geneva and wife of Aymé Levet, an apothecary and also a good citizen, a very pious woman and able to read very well, was persuaded by her sister-in-law to go hear Fromment preach. Touched by the sermon, she went home to read the New Testament for three days, was converted to Protestantism, and then converted many other women by her speech and example.[95]

> When she found herself in a gathering where there was no minister present, those assembled had her explain the Scripture, for one could not find a person more gifted with graces of the Lord. . . . Leaving behind all her pomps, . . . she applied her possessions to the poor, principally those of the household of faith, and those who had been cast out for the truth, taking them into her house.[96]

Claudine Levet persuaded several other rich women to give up their pomps, too, and shelter refugees. But after the gospel had been preached for a time, their charity cooled. Some of the women blamed this on the bad example of the foreigners or the "wives" of former priests or the wives of ministers.[97]

Fromment recounts that after his first preaching in town, he was sheltered by the Levet family. Mobs threw rocks at their windows and mud in their shop, destroying their drugs; Sister Jeanne also tells of such an episode.[98] Aymé Levet is mentioned as one who returned the belongings of those whose homes were looted in the struggle with the Bernese in 1536.[99]

From Fromment's account as well as Sister Jeanne's one can conclude that Claudine Levet was preaching in public assemblies. There is no suggestion these were merely assemblies of women. Both accounts reflect respect by Protestant men for Madame Levet's preaching, her gifts of grace, and her effectiveness in converting people to the new faith.

There is an intriguing reference in Fromment's account of the warm charity of the early days of the Reformation that deacons, men and women, made inquiries and distributed aid where there was need.[100] This term "deacon" may be used only quite generally to mean those who served the needs of others, or it may have its full significance. But it is fascinating in view of Calvin's later discussions of women deacons to hear that men and women are spoken of together in carrying out this diaconal work in the earliest days of the Genevan Reformation, before Calvin arrived.

Davis recounts that in the French city of Nîmes thirty years later, a Reformed consistory called on four women to gather alms for the poor.[101] These women are not spoken of as deaconesses. But a similar task may have been carried out by those women.

In the case of the second woman preacher mentioned by Sister Jeanne, Marie Dentière, it is possible to go beyond the information offered by her chronicle and that of the pastor, Fromment. Other sources report that Fromment is the husband of Dentière, and that she herself is a published author. Her booklet on the Genevan Reformation, *The War and Deliverance of the City of Geneva,* published there in 1536, has been called by its editor "the oldest literary production coming out of Geneva from a Protestant pen."[102] Recounting in lively style the events of the struggle of the Genevese from 1504 to 1536, Dentière affirms her faith in the God who works his will victoriously out of the midst of the people's despair, without regard to their merit, so that honor and glory be rendered to God by all. The liberation of the Jews from Egyptian slavery figures prominently in perspective.[103]

Dentière's second publication was a booklet addressed to Marguerite, Queen of Navarre, consisting of a covering letter to the Queen, a "Defense of Women," and "A Very Useful Letter," published in Geneva in 1539.[104] Fromment explains that Marguerite had inquired of Dentière, a *commère* (godmother or, by extension, a good friend), about the exile of the Genevan ministers, one of whom was Calvin.[105] Dentière's frank expressions of disrespect for the current ministers in Geneva and others known to Marguerite, along with Dentière's implied support for the exiled Calvin, created a scandal in Geneva, leading to the arrest of the printer, the confiscation of remaining stock of the edition, and the imposition of censorship.[106]

Of special interest here is Dentière's view of women's freedom in the church. It seems that she has so internalized the Reformed teaching of the freedom of the Christian and has so situated herself in the biblical view of God's liberating work in history that she feels called to write and speak, knowing full well that these roles are neither ecclesiastically nor culturally approved for women. One notes, for example, that both her volumes were published anonymously, though the second states that she is a woman.

Dentière ends her covering letter to Marguerite with the plea that she intercede with her brother, the king of France, to end divisions, for what God has revealed to women as well as men should not be hidden.

> Although it is not permitted to us [women] to preach in public assemblies and churches, it is nonetheless not forbidden to write and admonish one another, in all love. Not only for you, my Lady, have I wished to write this letter, but also to give courage to other women held in captivity, in order that they may not all fear being exiled from their country, relatives and friends, like myself, for the word of God . . . , that they may from now on not be tormented and afflicted in themselves but rather rejoicing, consoled, and excited to follow the

truth, which is the gospel of Jesus Christ. Till now this gospel has
been hidden so that one did not dare to say a word about it, and it
seemed that women should read and understand nothing in the holy
writings. This is the principal cause, my Lady, which moved me to
write you, hoping in God that in the future women will not be so
much despised as in the past . . . throughout all the world.[107]

Given the literary device of Dentière that she is writing as a
woman to women, conceivably to make the publication less offensive, one could wonder whether the references here to women
are not meant to be read simply as references to Protestants. But
her other writings also have a feminist quality. The style of her
history of reform in Geneva is noticeably "inclusive" (to use a
twentieth-century term), including Sarah as well as Abraham,
Elizabeth as well as Zechariah, and many references to her concern about contemporary women. And her brief "Defense of
Women"[108] is very much in the genre of Agrippa of Nettesheim's
"Declamation on the Nobility of Women." She recounts the significant women of the Bible, pointing out that it was not women who
betrayed Jesus or were false prophets, or were deceived by false
prophets, who invented ceremonies and false doctrines, but men.
When Dentière points to the Samaritan woman as one of the
greatest of the preachers of Jesus, and when she recalls that Jesus
revealed himself after the resurrection first to women and commanded them to preach his resurrection to others, we recall
Calvin's careful explanations to the effect that these women told
their good news to their friends, but were not really "preachers"![109]
Dentière concludes:

> If God then has given graces to some good women, revealing to them
> by his Holy Scriptures something holy and good, will they not dare to
> write, speak, or declare it one to another? . . . Ah! It would be too au-
> dacious to wish to stop them from doing it. As for us, it would be too
> foolish to hide the talent which God has given us.[110]

Calvin certainly must have known that women had been preaching in Geneva before his arrival and that their gifts were respected.
Therefore it seems likely that his comment that Paul's advice for
women to be silent is to be confined "to what is fitting in a properly
organized congregation"[111] is a way of expressing approval of the
freedom of the early Protestants to permit women to preach in
their gatherings. The certainty that Calvin could have experienced
a positive tradition of women's public—though unofficial—ministry in Geneva also helps to support the judgment that Calvin is
genuinely open to exceptions to the normal rule of women's

subordination. Those who heard Calvin preach knew that there were indeed more recent examples of women endowed with special gifts than just the biblical ones. But despite the skills of these women preachers, they must have been found wanting by the high standards of theological education the Geneva company of pastors demanded of its preachers. In fact during the early years of the Reformation no native Genevese at all was chosen a pastor; all the pastors were refugees. The women lost out to the tightening up of institutions as the Reformation was firmly established. Special roles for women were permissible during an "emergency" situation but no longer tolerated when the new order was instituted.

Is there any evidence of an unusually favorable attitude toward women in Calvin's Geneva? William Monter has done a careful study of women's social situation in Geneva from 1550 to 1800. He concludes that the consistory in Calvin's years, though generally strict, was on the whole very egalitarian, treating men and women alike. In fact their fairness caused many complaints from the men, who were no longer benefiting from the traditional double standard. Only for infanticide were women alone punished. In the case of witchcraft, "Calvinist Geneva had an unusually low conviction rate for this crime, and it punished men accused of witchcraft relatively more severely than women."[112] But the education available for girls, though probably improving basic literacy to some degree, did not permit women in the coming years to play a significant role in cultural life. Genevan women authors, for example, were conspicuously absent after Sister Jeanne and Marie Dentière until the nineteenth century.[113]

Calvin's view in relation to sixteenth-century Protestant confessions. It is important for perspective to have some sense of how Protestant confessions of the sixteenth century deal with the question of freedom with respect to Paul's advice concerning women's proper roles.

First, we should point out that most of the Protestant confessions of the time discuss what is called "human tradition." When this term refers, as it usually does, to ecclesiastical laws seen to be without warrant in Scripture or which are perceived to be contrary to Scripture and which have been made binding upon the consciences of Christians, laws such as those concerning celibacy or fast days, they are regularly declared by the Protestant confessions to be useless and ungodly.[114] On the other hand, approval is usually given to rites that are useful to the peace, unity, and good order of the church without being considered binding on the conscience, as we have heard Calvin explain.[115]

In three confessions, all of them very early chronologically, the advice of Paul concerning conduct in church, such as women covering their heads, is referred to as an example of salutary and useful tradition, but still not binding so as to be necessary to salvation or an occasion for sin unless others were offended. Examples are the Augsburg Confession of the Lutherans of 1530, written by Melanchthon, the Tetrapolitan Confession of Bucer of 1530, and the Geneva Confession of 1536, possibly written by Farel and edited by Calvin. The Augsburg and Tetrapolitan Confessions explicitly mention the question of women covering their heads; the Geneva Confession does not. None of the three specifically mentions women's silence in the church. Calvin certainly knew both the Augsburg Confession and the Tetrapolitan Confession during his years in Strasbourg and probably before going to Geneva, and he publicly expressed his approval of the Augsburg Confession.[116] So he would have felt himself in the mainstream of Protestant thought in his general treatment of Paul's advice as not binding on the conscience. The Tetrapolitan Confession alone of these three confessions also includes the idea that the traditions could be updated to changing circumstances: "Many such the Church even today justly observes, and according to occasion frames anew."[117] Melanchthon's *Apology of the Augsburg Confession* of 1531 seems to have no specific reference to women covering their heads or keeping silence.

We can conclude, then, that Calvin's view of women's freedom in the church stems from Luther only in the very broad matters where Luther brought the priesthood of all believers to bear on women's role, such as the dignity of marriage, basic education, participation in public worship as a lay person. From the humanists, especially Bucer, Calvin has drawn still more concerning women's freedom in the church.

But I have found so far no Reformer other than Calvin who specifically includes Paul's advice for women to be silent in the church among the *adiaphora* where the church should be open to change. Calvin's choice to add this reference to the ones he found on women covering their heads in Melanchthon and Bucer—and to continue to include it through all the editions of the *Institutes*—would seem to be related to his experience in French humanistic culture of the period, where women's public roles were frequently discussed and experienced. Calvin seems to have heard the early sixteenth-century dialogue on women's rights and concluded in principle that women could be given the right to speak in church—a symbol for public teaching and preaching roles.

This may explain why, to the best of my knowledge, Calvin never explicitly discusses the fact that women were preaching publicly in Geneva before the Reformation was established. He admits that there are times when women need to speak publicly, and therefore he has no desire to condemn that practice in the days when proper pastors were not available. But given the changed ecclesiastical context since the establishment of the Reformation and the social upheaval of his own time,[118] he no longer finds it appropriate to encourage the more radical freedom in the church that women had earlier experienced. He is trying to protect a social order that is already in danger of disintegrating, he believes.

So I think Calvin would not thunder at Madame Levet and Madame Fromment, calling down the wrath of God upon them. Rather, I think he would assure them that greater freedom for women in the church is a movement in the direction of the equality of the kingdom that will come someday—but not yet! Still, the practical consequence in either case for the women of Calvin's day would have been very much the same: silence.

6
Freedom
in Obedience

"Peter pronounces those people free who serve God. . . . This is the purpose of our freedom, that we may be more prompt and more unencumbered for the service of God."[1] In this passage from the commentary on 1 Peter, Calvin echoes the theme of his introduction to the Ten Commandments: "The Lord means that they have been freed from miserable bondage that they may, in obedience and readiness to serve, worship him as the author of their freedom."[2]

We come now to the third part of Christian freedom that Calvin set forth in the *Institutes*. We have examined the first two parts: rising above all law-righteousness and embracing God's mercy alone for assurance of justification; recognizing those things which are in themselves "indifferent." We will now discuss the third: willing obedience to the law as God's will.

The whole mainstream of the Reformation sees ethics as a response to justification, not the cause of it. Justification is offered by the mere liberality of God and is in no way dependent on human merit. Christ's work of satisfaction for sin requires no human supplement.[3] Luther most often seems to speak of a free and spontaneous outpouring of love and service to the neighbor in gratitude for what Christ has done. The service is a consequence of justification and is directed to the neighbor because God has no need of our service. But in the passages from Calvin with which we began this chapter there is a subtle shift: Christian freedom is given in order that we may serve God more readily.[4] And in the description of the third aspect of Christian freedom was the other characteristically Calvinist note: willing obedience to the *law* as

God's will. This is the so-called "third use of the law"[5] as guidance for the Christian life. Christians who have been liberated from the obligations of the law by Christ's work freely study God's law in order to understand God's will and to reshape their lives in voluntary obedience to it. Calvin sees the liberation of the conscience in Christian freedom as a powerful aid to Christians in their voluntary service to God and to the neighbor which the law reveals as the will of God. Calvin takes great pains in his commentaries, where a passage might possibly be interpreted as implying justification by merits, to point out that the gospel teaches otherwise. Though it is grace which saves, there is, however, some consolation for Christians to know that God will receive human works, inadequate though they are.[6]

Despite the care with which Calvin frames his statements, through the years he has repeatedly been called a "legalist," usually in a pejorative fashion, by Protestants who do not understand his third use of the law. So it is fascinating to see a historian of Judaism, Salo Baron, comment in a rather positive tone that Calvin's attitudes toward the law are remarkably similar to those of the rabbis of his age. Their teachings "had great affinity to those of a reformer who had, to all intents and purposes, abandoned Pauline antinomianism in favor of Old Testament legalism."[7] The term "legalism" here obviously has a very different sense than above and carries with it a love of the law. Baron points particularly to Calvin's description of the function of law to warn of duty and arouse zeal for holiness, his stress on the intention behind the act, and his treatment of the prohibition of imagery.[8] It appears that Baron has grasped Calvin's third use of the law, but not its context in relation to the first use, since he sets Calvin squarely over against Paul.

Attempts to explain the reason for Calvin's adoption of the third use of the law vary. We must remember that "second-generation" Reformers like Calvin had a difficult apologetic task in the domain of ethics. Roman Catholics and many Protestants, including especially the Anabaptists, were agreed that Luther's Reformation had failed to bring about any very visible improvement in the moral life of Christendom. Calvin therefore feels a special need to demonstrate that the doctrine of justification by faith is not only compatible with concern for morality but will even increase moral sensitivity. Here we find Calvin on common ground with other humanistically oriented Reformers. It is often pointed out that the humanists among the Reformers have placed more emphasis on sanctification than Luther did.[9] Bouwsma sees a similar connection to humanism. He says of Calvin: "Not the least of his contributions to the needs of the age was . . . a system of both external constraints and internalized discipline that supplied a practical substitute for the discredited metaphysical structures that had previously been a source of guidance and comfort."[10] Heiko Oberman looks rather to the role of the Spirit in Calvin's thought.

> Whereas for Luther faith is effectuated by the *verbum Dei* [word of God], the presence of Christ as the mode of the preached word, from Karlstadt, Zwingli, and Bucer to the most explicit statements with Calvin, faith as *operatio spiritus sancti* [work of the Holy Spirit] is a call to action. Faith is not, as Trent would put it, the *initium iustitiae* [beginning of righteousness] but it is the *initium regni* [beginning of the kingdom], the kingdom as the presence of Christ in the mode of the ecclesio-political community, implying the impatient reordering of creation, church and society.[11]

This last suggestion very helpfully relates this discussion of obedience to the comments in chapter 1, above, on Christian freedom as the sign of the kingdom. The Spirit energizes Christians to make the signs of the kingdom visible already here on earth; obedient service requires reformation.

Within this kingdom of Christ God is to be properly honored. Calvin explicitly analyzes the honoring of God in the Geneva Catechism of 1545 and uses a parallel structure to explain the First Commandment in the *Institutes*.[12] We will here follow the Catechism. The right way of honoring (*honorandi*) God is:

> To put all our trust in him; to study to worship [*colere*] him all our lives, by obeying his will; to call upon him, whenever any need impels us, seeking in him salvation and whatever good things can be desired; and lastly, to acknowledge him with both heart and mouth to be the only author of all good things.[13]

Here at the beginning of the Catechism Calvin speaks of "honoring" as well as "worshiping" God. But consistently throughout the rest of the Catechism he speaks of the various ways of "worshiping" God.[14] Obedience to the Decalogue is as much "worship" as the invocation of God. Translators obscure the consistency by rendering *colere* (which means, in respect to God, "to honor, reverence, or worship") in some places as "to worship," in others as "to serve." Modern people are accustomed to speaking of worship as service, but most have lost Calvin's sense that service in the sense of obedience to the law is also worship. John Greenleaf Whittier has caught Calvin's spirit with his line, "Each loving life a psalm of gratitude."[15]

Calvin in a sermon on the nativity of Christ reflects on the angels' song, "Glory to God in the highest, and on earth peace to humanity: good will."[16] He explains that sinners' mouths are closed, shut up by the anguish of remorse, not knowing whether God loves or hates them, till they feel his goodness and love declared to them by God himself, who reveals himself to be always their father. But then:

> Let us learn not to have at all a dead and lazy faith, but let us be
> stirred up to bless the name of God when we see that he has made
> available to us the great treasures of his mercy; and let the mouth do
> its duty on the one hand and let our whole life respond. For there is
> the true hymn, that all dedicate themselves to the service of God,
> knowing that, since he has bought us so dearly, it is right that all our
> thoughts and our works should be applied to that use, that his name
> be praised.[17]

Trust is the necessary starting point for worshiping God because of its liberating effect on the Christian person. The word "trust" in Reformation language is often used as a definition of faith, and in the Catechism Calvin explains trust in terms of a saving knowledge of God's good favor and mercy in Jesus Christ;[18] trust is a gift of the Holy Spirit. Trust opens a free and confident relationship with God in strong contrast to Calvin's description of the sinner's anxious, "shut-up," restricted, fearful relationship to God.

In explaining the benefits of Christ's work to the Christian, Calvin says that its only purpose was the sharing of the Spirit's gifts with Christians. Christ's kingdom "sets free our consciences for pious and holy living" and provides spiritual riches; and we are "armed with strength sufficient to overcome the perpetual enemies of our souls, sin, the flesh, the devil, and the world."[19] From Christ's priestly office we receive boldness of access to God and become Christ's "colleagues in the priesthood," offering ourselves entirely to God.[20] From Christ's prophetic office we receive true knowledge of God and instruction in truth and become "household disciples of God." These offices were conferred on Christ in order that he would "transfuse their strength and fruit into those who are his."[21]

It is striking how regularly Calvin identifies enlivening, courage, strength, boldness with the state of Christian freedom as a sign of the Spirit's activity. The Christian is never struck down by God because of sin nor burdened by troubles and misfortune without being immediately raised up in order to march forward courageously in the service of God. In a noteworthy passage of the commentary on Job, Calvin discusses the purpose of preaching, insisting vigorously that it must address the particular needs of those to whom the preacher is speaking. But he especially emphasizes that

> the word of God is to teach the ignorant, to fortify the weak. . . . It exhorts those who are slack and . . . cold . . . , it awakens those who are asleep in their faults . . . , but still more . . . it revivifies the dead. . . . Let us note well, then, that the word of God will be treated as it should when it will give us courage to walk, fortify us in our feebleness, and render us agile when we would have had broken legs; when, instead of being deprived of all strength as before, it would make us strong and robust; but it should give us life when we would otherwise be as good as dead.[22]

Calvin stresses particularly the power of the gospel to give courage and strength when he speaks to women, probably because of the general cultural assumption that they are weaker and more timid by nature than men. Writing to women imprisoned in Paris for their faith, he referred to the women at the tomb:

> If he then so honored women, and endowed them with so much courage, do you think he has less power now, or that his purposes have changed? How many thousands of women have there been who have spared neither their blood nor their lives to maintain the name of Jesus Christ and announce his reign! Has not God caused their martyrdom to fructify? Has their faith not obtained the glory of the world as well as that of martyrs? . . . Have we not still, before our eyes, examples of how God works daily by their testimony, and confounds his enemies in such a manner that there is no preaching of such efficacy as the fortitude and perseverance which they possess in confessing the name of Christ?[23]

In the study that Charmarie Blaisdell has done of Calvin's correspondence with noblewomen in France, comparing it with that of Ignatius Loyola, she indicates that Calvin deals with these women primarily as nobility rather than as women. "Calvin seemed less paternal and, perhaps, less condescending in his attitude toward his female correspondents than Loyola, exhorting them to firm up their backbones and get on with the work of God, including the propagation of the faith."[24] The trust with which God is to be honored leads to courageous freedom of action.

The second aspect of worship is the invocation of God whenever the Christian feels in need. One can invoke God with confidence despite a sense of sinfulness because the Spirit incites such boldness and because of God's promises.[25] In praying the Lord's Prayer,

"Thy will be done," Calvin says, "I desire such inclination to obedience among human beings that they will all yield themselves to God completely in voluntary subjection."[26] Christians freely call upon God and offer themselves in willing service.

Third, the section of the Catechism devoted to acknowledging God with heart and mouth as the author of all good things is essentially a discussion of the Word to be appropriated privately through study, corporately through public worship, and finally sacramentally through baptism and the Lord's Supper.[27] This aspect of the worship of God has an element of witness and public confession within it. One of the purposes of the sacraments, Calvin explains, is their use as "marks and badges of our profession. For by using them, we profess our faith before others and testify that we are in entire agreement with the Christian religion."[28]

One remembers here the deep disappointment Calvin experienced in those who believed in the Reformed understanding of the gospel but would not publicly make their confession by joining in worship and the fellowship of the Lord's Supper. He called them the Nicodemites.[29] Calvin was very conscious of the risk of persecution many would incur in making such a profession, especially in France, but continued to urge believers to make their confession and support the growing Protestant movement. Though it is striking that so little is said in this context about such public witness, one must remember that the Catechism was intended for the people of Geneva, a city that had already declared itself as Reformed.

In a sermon on the passion story in John's Gospel, Calvin takes up the theme of Nicodemus, who was too fearful to come to Jesus by day. But after Jesus' death he came with Joseph, another fearful and secret disciple, who had claimed Jesus' body, to embalm it. These men through the power of the Spirit were changed and given a remarkable new courage to declare their faith.[30] One cannot help connecting this sermon with Calvin's struggle with the Nicodemites of his own day.

It is also surprising that in this context of the Catechism Calvin says so little about gratitude. Elsewhere gratitude is an often-repeated theme: service to God represents gratitude, impiety represents ingratitude.[31] Christians should learn gratitude for all God's blessings.

Calvin sees the world God created as designed to provide for the needs of all human beings bountifully and abundantly, with a profusion of natural wealth.[32] Commenting on the description of this bountiful aspect of the creation in Genesis, Calvin finds a lesson on the need for stewardship of the land: one should hand down one's fields to posterity in as good a condition as one received them or better.[33] He implies that one would be ungrateful not to exercise such good stewardship of the creation given to humanity for its benefit.

Calvin summarizes these themes in a passage of the *Institutes* that François Wendel has compared to Luther's Catechism.[34]

> Whenever we call God the Creator of heaven and earth, let us at the same time bear in mind that the dispensation of all those things which he has made is in his own hand and power and that we are indeed his children, whom he has received into his faithful protection to nourish and educate. We are therefore to await the fullness of all good things from him alone and to trust completely that he will never leave us destitute of what we need for salvation, and to hang our hopes on none but him! We are therefore, also, to petition him for whatever we desire; and we are to recognize as a blessing from him, and thankfully to acknowledge, every benefit that falls to our share. So, invited by the great sweetness of his beneficence and goodness, let us study to love and serve him with all our heart.[35]

We come now to the remaining aspect of the worship of God, obedience to the will of God as shown in the law. Christian freedom for Calvin implies abrogation of ceremonial law; but there is a new relation to moral law rather than an abrogation of it. "To be Christians under the law of grace does not mean to wander unbridled outside the law, but to be engrafted in Christ, by whose grace we are free of the curse of the law, and by whose Spirit we have the law engraved upon our hearts."[36] In the Christian life knowledge of the law induces humility, encourages seeking strength from the Lord, and provides a mark at which to aim in spiritual growth.[37]

In an exploration of the broad topic of obedience, it will be necessary to choose an example on which to focus the discussion; we will sketch the outlines of Calvin's understanding of one's duty to the neighbor. In summarizing the second table of the law in the Catechism, Calvin explains that "neighbors" are not only relatives and friends but even persons unknown to us and enemies. "They are certainly joined by that bond by which God gathers the whole human race at once. But it is a tie, sacred and inviolable, which cannot be loosed by the depravity of anyone."[38] The same point is made strongly in the commentary on Acts 13. "People are not born for themselves alone, but the whole human race is interconnected, linked together with a holy bond."[39] Calvin notes that in the Lord's Prayer Christians address God corporately as "Our Father" and pray in common for their daily bread.[40] The image of God in creation was given to Adam and Eve together. God created one couple so that all human beings proceeding from that couple would recognize one another as one flesh.[41] Even the impious who are ungrateful to God and stand outside the household of faith receive gifts of learning and skills that are useful for the common welfare.[42]

With this vision of faith Christians should perceive the ethical demand placed upon them by the presence of the image of God in all human beings, regardless of their sinfulness. Though the image is clearest in the restored "household of faith," it exists in all persons.

> Therefore, whatever human being you now meet who needs your aid, you have no reason to refuse to help the person. Say "He is a stranger"; but the Lord has given him a mark that ought to be familiar to you, by virtue of the fact that God forbids you to despise your own flesh. Say, "He is contemptible and worthless"; but the Lord shows him to be one to whom he has deigned to give the beauty of his image. Say that you owe nothing for any service of his; but God, as it were, has put him in his own place in order that you may recognize toward him the many and great benefits with which God has bound you to himself. . . . The image of God, which recommends the person to you, is worthy of your giving yourself and all your possessions. . . . Assuredly there is but one way in which to achieve what is not merely difficult but utterly against human nature: to love those who hate us. . . . It is that we remember not to consider people's evil intentions but to look upon the image of God in them, which cancels and effaces their transgressions, and with its beauty and dignity allures us to love and embrace them.[43]

We see then that one very fundamental element in Calvin's view of the proper ordering of society and the proper way to do one's duty to the neighbor is his biblical understanding of the image of God as a corporate one, belonging to all humanity. This surely underlies also his vision of the catholicity of the church[44] and his development of corporate styles of church governance and pastoral care.

Still another element in Calvin's corporate vision of society is a more broadly cultural one. Scholars today are pointing out that Renaissance humanism was placing more emphasis on the social values of human community in the early sixteenth century than previously.[45] Many humanists were now taking up more active roles involving social change rather than purely scholarly ones.[46] But behind the Renaissance values are the corporate urban values of medieval cities which some scholars describe as a vision of "a sacred society."[47] Bernd Moeller has sparked enormous discussion and lively debate about the relation of the medieval cities to the growth of the Reformation, a debate we cannot enter here without digression. In his study of *Imperial Cities and the Reformation,* he does not of course discuss Calvin's Geneva at all. But one can see strong parallels in Geneva to his description of the process of reformation of the imperial cities, including the direct participation of the community in the decision to become Reformed, the community oath of the citizens, and the conviction that this community decision once taken required conformity by all the citizens.[48] There are also striking parallels in Geneva to his description of the style of life of those Reformed imperial cities: austerity of worship services, energetic moral reform and civil discipline, public charity and public education, with marked involvement of lay persons.[49] Though some of these parallels are surely a reflection of a common Reformation theology, we must not overlook the social structure and ideals of the medieval city—which in their turn also reflect theology—in our effort to understand Calvin's vision of social relationships. Like Zwingli and Bullinger, Calvin was trying to adapt evangelical teaching to the life of an urban community with a strong tradition of mutual responsibility among the citizens.

The Geneva in which Calvin was preaching was a small and crowded city, attacked and harassed periodically by troops from neighboring Catholic territories, and pressed to overflowing by a steady influx of Protestant refugees. Since the population within the city was growing, yet the outlying suburbs and agricultural lands could not be secured, supplies of basic commodities were often restricted. There was tension between the old Genevan families and the refugees who were changing the life of the city.[50]

Under these circumstances Calvin's discussions of the relation of Christian freedom to the use of temporal goods can be seen to have a very immediate and practical importance. Though one is free in conscience to enjoy all the good things that God has created, one will not do so at the expense of the welfare of a neighbor made in the image of God. The rich should see in the poor person before their eyes the Son of God, to whom it would be a terrible sacrilege to refuse anything.[51]

Calvin reminds the rich that what they possess has been given them in trust for their needs and the needs of others; they will be held accountable for their stewardship. Commenting on 2 Corinthians 8:13–17, where Paul urges the Corinthians to share their abundance with those in want, so that there may be "equality,"

Calvin does not think this means mathematical equality; rather, it means the sharing of the members of the church "in proportion to their gifts and needs," since all that they have comes from God. Recalling God's provision of manna in the wilderness, he comments:

> The Lord has not prescribed to us an omer or any other measure for the food we have each day, but he has commended to us frugality and temperance and has forbidden anyone from going to excess because of abundance. Thus those who have riches, whether inherited or won by their own industry and labor, are to keep in mind that what is left over is meant not for intemperance or luxury but for relieving the needs of the brothers. . . . I acknowledge indeed that we are not bound to such an equality as would make it wrong for the rich to live more elegantly than the poor; but there must be such an equality that nobody is hungry and nobody hoards abundance at another's expense.[52]

He believes God has provided bountifully for all, if people will only share God's gifts.

Calvin reminds his readers: "We are not our own. . . . We are God's. . . . We seek not the things that are ours but those which are of the Lord's will and will serve to advance his glory."[53] This perspective frees Christians to be self-forgetful and open to the neighbor's need. Those who give should not merely be cheerful but "put themselves in the place of the one whom they see in need of their assistance, and pity the person's ill fortune as if they themselves experienced and bore it," without any concern for gratitude from the receiver. The only limit which should be set in kindness to those in need is the end of one's resources; that is the limit set by the rule of love.[54]

Those who hold positions of public authority, like magistrates and pastors, must also realize that their authority should not be self-serving. Hierarchical authority in society has been given by God for service, for the common good.[55]

In the context of Paul's discussion of Christian liberty in 1 Corinthians 10:23–24, Calvin confronts the tension between two aspects of freedom: one's freedom of conscience in indifferent things and one's freedom to serve.

> Do you mean that something which God, in other circumstances, allows ceases to be permissible if it is not to the advantage of our neighbors? For if that is the case, then our freedom would be in the control of other human beings. Give careful thought to what Paul is actually saying, and you will realize that, after all, your freedom is not

impaired in the slightest when you accommodate yourself to your
neighbors, but in fact all that is restricted is your exercise of it. For
Paul agrees that it is lawful, but he says that it must not be used if it
does not make for the upbuilding of people. ... But just as the law of
love wants us to love our neighbors as ourselves, so it summons us to
caring for their welfare. Finally, the apostle does not explicitly forbid
individuals to think about their own interests; but he does not want
them to be so much bound up in them that they will not give up part
of what is their right whenever the welfare of their brothers demands
it.[56]

The same theme is taken up in the *Institutes:*

Our freedom is not given against our feeble neighbors, for love
makes us their servant in all things; rather it is given in order that,
having peace with God in our hearts, we may also live at peace with
human beings.[57]

We cannot conclude our sketch of Calvin's understanding of
freedom in obedience without lifting up the theme of joy in service.
Obedient service to God, Calvin thinks, will necessarily bring with
it struggle against poverty, enemies, unbelievers who despise the
faith, and ignominy. But in a sermon preached at the Lord's
Supper on Christmas Day, he rejoices in the midst of all these
troubles in the peace that God's service brings through the faith
that God is in and with Christians: through the incarnation where
God was made a human person, through Christ's presence in the
Sacrament, and through the vivifying power of the Holy Spirit. If
they ask nothing more than to glorify their God, Christ will bless
their miseries. "And there where worldly people are confounded in
their triumphs, inasmuch as they take pleasure only in fighting
against God, let our true joy be in serving God in all fear and
humility and in devoting ourselves entirely to his obedience."[58]

In the service of God in the world, one is joyfully freed from
selfishness, fear, and the power of evil and given a peaceful heart.
Voluntary obedience to God's will is itself an aspect of Christian
freedom; it is made possible by the Holy Spirit's enlivening and
strengthening of the Christian person and constitutes a sign of the
presence of Christ's kingdom.

Now that we have examined in succeeding chapters the various
aspects of Christian freedom that Calvin identifies, we return to
reflect upon some of the many questions that have been raised by
the reading of Calvin along the way.

How can a Christian be free if God is constantly intervening in
human affairs to carry out God's plan in history? As Calvin puts it

in the *Institutes,* "God, whenever he wills to make way for his providence, bends and turns human wills even in external things; nor are they so free to choose that God's will does not rule over their freedom. Whether you will or not, daily experience compels you to realize that your mind is guided by God's prompting rather than by your own freedom to choose."[59]

How can one who speaks so much of freedom in "indifferent things," and who insists on respecting the freedom of Christians in other cities to differ from Geneva in its practices, be willing to tolerate so little diversity in Geneva itself?

If the church represents the inbreaking kingdom of Christ where equality among all persons prevails, why should there be any hierarchy in the church? Why, if women's silence in church is an "indifferent matter," cannot women speak if their consciences demand it?

If Christians are free of the power of evil and transformed into new beings, why does the church need so much discipline of its members?

Though these are modern questions, we have seen that they are also questions raised in Calvin's day, questions to which he made at least some attempt to provide a careful answer. But in dealing with particular questions it is easy to lose sight of the broader perspectives. So we shall attempt to draw together Calvin's major themes and grasp his fundamental perspective on these matters.

The heart of Christian freedom as Calvin understands it is the experience of transformation by the Holy Spirit, an experience he believes the philosophers simply do not understand. In Romans 12:1–2 Christians are taught not to be conformed to this world but to be transformed.

> We are consecrated and dedicated to God in order that we may thereafter think, speak, meditate, and do nothing except to his glory. . . . We are not our own: let not our reason nor our will, therefore, sway our plans and deeds. . . . We are God's. . . . While it is the first entrance to life, all philosophers were ignorant of this transformation, which Paul calls "renewal of the mind." For they set up reason alone as the ruling principle in human beings and think that it alone should be listened to; to it alone, in short, they entrust the conduct of life. But the Christian philosophy bids reason give way to, submit and subject itself to, the Holy Spirit so that the persons themselves may no longer live but hear Christ living and reigning within them.[60]

The Spirit creates new hearts and minds that delight in serving God. In receiving a new heart that willingly obeys the will of God, the Christian experiences true freedom. To be bent and turned by God away from evil to the purposes of God is not experienced by the Christian, Calvin thinks, as coercion but rather as liberation. To understand oneself as predestined by God to participation in the kingdom is not a cause for resignation but a spur to energetic pursuit of good. "If election has as its goal holiness of life, it ought rather to arouse and goad us eagerly to set our mind upon it than to serve as a pretext for doing nothing."[61]

The willing quality of this self-offering to God is perhaps epitomized by Calvin's familiar symbol of a heart aflame on a hand stretched out to God. He also speaks in his writings of the love of God inflaming hearts to devotion and self-giving.[62] This is the work of the Holy Spirit.

Since Calvin understands God as a God of freedom, the experience of Christian freedom is an aspect of participation in divine life. The Spirit's imparting of freedom to Christians to serve God willingly as well as freedom from the power of evil, of sin and death, is one aspect of the inbreaking of Christ's kingdom into the world in the community of the church, the members of Christ's body. Here there is also freedom from hierarchies of class, nation, and sex. Calvin stresses, however, that this is a spiritual kingdom. Insofar as the church continues to live in a sinful world and even Christians continue to struggle with sin, there must continue to be hierarchical authority, preferably corporate in nature, to hold the church accountable to God's word through discipline. But church structures and laws are human creations and are not eternal, but rather subject to change as necessary for faithfulness to the Word of God and for the edification of God's people.

Because Calvin understands God to be not only free but also just, Calvin sees the Christian as called in freedom over against human authorities to transform the unjust human structures of church and society to make them reflect more nearly the pattern of the kingdom of Christ which is already present in the church. We have hardly done more than call attention to Calvin's biblical passion for social justice. Here is the source of enormous energy for social transformation.

Calvin clearly worries, however, about the problem of controlling that reforming energy. Many of the calls to reform that he hears seem to him to be too radical for the moment or poorly designed, dangerous to the somewhat unstable situation of society in the mid-sixteenth century. Morély's desire for a more democratic structuring of the church and the concern of some humanists to free women from subordination to men are two examples we have touched upon where others saw the implications of Christian freedom differently than Calvin. Calvin's awareness of the depth of human sinfulness makes him very cautious about immediate radical reform of the structures of society. Yet there is some evidence that he was conscious of the provisional nature of contemporary administrative arrangements in Geneva and open to experimentation elsewhere, as well as to future change, whereas his immediate successors tended to be more doctrinaire and less flexible.[63] Calvin's persistent teaching that the silence of women in church is a matter of time-bound apostolic advice rather than divine law for all time is an example of his openness to major change in the future.

Since Calvin understands God to be not only free and just but also loving, Calvin admires the way his biblical God, perfectly free of all constraint, chooses to impose self-limitations in dealing with the people of God so that human beings can understand what God is like. God's incarnation in human form and God's gift of the sacraments are two examples he finds of such accommodation to the human condition by a free and loving God. Calvin seems to suggest that this gratuitous accommodation by God to humanity is mirrored in the voluntary accommodation of one human being to another. Though freed by Christ's work from any obligation under the law, Christians nonetheless voluntarily share their possessions with those in need and accept discipline and restrictions on their conduct out of concern for the common good of all who bear God's image. Calvin's understanding of Christian freedom seems more strongly rooted in the context of social life—the life of the city and the life of the church—than in the context of individual existence, though concern for the freedom of the individual conscience is far from absent. The coexistence in Calvin of the strong focus on Christian freedom and the stress on corporate discipline can perhaps best be comprehended in this light.

Calvin willingly sets aside the vision of freedom offered by the philosophers in favor of his view of Christian freedom: liberation by Christ's work from the power of sin and evil and the anguished conscience in order to worship God, to devote oneself freely and energetically to making the kingdom of Christ manifest in the world, freedom to participate in history in the Holy Spirit's creation of the new society envisioned and empowered by God.

Notes

1: The Foundation of Christian Freedom

1. *Inst.* II, xi, 9.
2. 1536 *Inst.* 6, 1, *O.S.* I, 223–224.
3. 1536 *Inst.* 6, 56, *O.S.* I, 280 (1 Cor. 7:23). Cf. *Inst.* III, xix, 14.
4. Quirinus Breen, *John Calvin: A Study in French Humanism,* p. 163.
5. Ford L. Battles, *A Computerized Concordance to Institutio christianae religionis, 1559,* Reel 3, words related to *libertas.*
6. T. H. L. Parker, *John Calvin: A Biography,* esp. pp. 51–53, 79–81, 153–155.
7. Steven Ozment, *The Age of Reform, 1250–1550: An Intellectual and Religious History of Late Medieval and Reformation Europe,* pp. 374, 379.
8. Steven Ozment, *The Reformation in the Cities: The Appeal of Protestantism to Sixteenth-Century Germany and Switzerland,* p. 164.
9. Ozment, *The Reformation in the Cities,* p. 165.
10. Cf. Breen, *John Calvin,* p. 164.
11. *Inst.* III, xix, 1.
12. *Inst.* III, xix, 2.
13. Ibid.
14. *Inst.* III, xix, 4.
15. *Inst.* III, xix, 5.
16. *Inst.* III, xix, 7.
17. Ibid.
18. *Inst.* III, xix, 9.
19. Ibid.
20. Ibid.
21. *Inst.* III, xix, 8.
22. *Inst.* III, xix, 12.
23. Ibid.

24. *Inst.* III, xix, 15.

25. *Inst.* III, xix, 14–16.

26. Martiñ Luther, *Von der Freiheit eines Christenmenschen,* 1520; *W.A.* 7, 3–38.

27. Edward F. Meylan, "The Stoic Doctrine of Indifferent Things and the Conception of Christian Liberty in Calvin's *Institutio religionis christianae," Romanic Review* 28 (1937), pp. 135–145. See Melanchthon, *C.R.* 21, 458–466 (1535 ed.).

28. Thomas Watson Street, "John Calvin on Adiaphora: An Exposition and Appraisal of His Theory and Practice" (Th.D. dissertation, Union Theological Seminary, New York, 1954), pp. 10–63. He says Calvin uses the Greek term rarely (p. 76).

29. See below, chapter 5, pp. 105–106.

30. *Inst.* IV, x, 1.

31. Street, p. 87.

32. Street, p. 325.

33. Street, p. 320.

34. Street, p. 167.

35. Street, p. 323.

36. Comm. Gen., *C.O.* 23, 39, 54–56, 61, 64.

37. *Inst.* II, ii, 5–8; II, iii, 5.

38. *Inst.* II, ii, 13–16.

39. *Inst.* II, ii, 20; II, iii, 6–8; III, iii, 9–10.

40. *Inst.* II, ii, 8.

41. *Inst.* II, viii, 15. Cf. *Inst.* II, xi, 9; II, xvi, 2; III, ii, 1; III, iii, 1; IV, x, 21, 23; Comm. Isa., *C.O.* 37, 93–94.

42. See Heiko A. Oberman, *The Harvest of Medieval Theology: Gabriel Biel and Late Medieval Nominalism,* chs. 2 and 4; François Wendel, *Calvin: The Origins and Development of His Religious Thought,* pp. 127–129; Kilian McDonnell, *John Calvin, the Church, and the Eucharist,* ch. 1. In contrast with Wendel and McDonnell who stress the influence of Scotus on Calvin, Ganoczy argues that Calvin was trained only in scholastic philosophy, not theology, and thus acquired from his training at Montaigu only a general dialectical structure of thought. Ganoczy believes Calvin may have subsequently acquired some elements of scholastic theology through his reading of Luther and others, but this remains of little significance. See Alexandre Ganoczy, *Le Jeune Calvin: Genèse et évolution de sa vocation réformatrice,* pp. 179–192.

43. *Inst.* II, xi, 14.

44. *Inst.* I, v, 8–9; I, xiv, 1, 3; I, xv, 8; I, xvi, 3; I, xvii, 1, 10–12; I, xviii, 4; II, v, 5; III, xxi, 1; III, xxiii, 2, 5; Comm. Job, *C.O.* 34, 339–343; Serm. I Tim., *C.O.* 53, 221.

45. Oberman, *Harvest,* chs. 6 and 7; E. Jane Dempsey Douglass, *Justification in Late Medieval Preaching: A Study of John Geiler of Keisersberg,* chs. 5 and 6. For a detailed discussion of the practice of confession and the varieties of teaching on attrition and contrition, see Thomas N. Tentler, *Sin and*

Confession on the Eve of the Reformation, ch. V.

46. *Inst.* III, xxi, 1; III, xxiv, 6.

47. *Inst.* III, iv, 3.

48. William J. Bouwsma, "Renaissance and Reformation: An Essay in Their Affinities and Connections," in *Luther and the Dawn of the Modern Era,* ed. Heiko A. Oberman, pp. 127–149, esp. pp. 139–140.

49. Ibid., pp. 132–134.

50. Ibid., pp. 135, 148. Cf. E. David Willis, "Rhetoric and Responsibility in Calvin's Theology," in *The Context of Contemporary Theology,* ed. Willis and Alexander J. McKelway, pp. 43–63. Cf. Bouwsma, "The Two Faces of Humanism, Stoicism, and Augustinianism in Renaissance Thought," in *Itinerarium Italicum: The Profile of the Italian Renaissance in the Mirror of Its European Transformations,* ed. Heiko A. Oberman with Thomas A. Brady, Jr., pp. 3–60, esp. pp. 38–39. Cf. Quirinus Breen, "St. Thomas and Calvin as Theologians: A Comparison," in *The Heritage of John Calvin,* ed. John H. Bratt, pp. 23–39. Some reservations to emphasizing the importance of Renaissance rhetoric in relation to Reformation preaching are expressed by Bengt Haegglund, "Renaissance and Reformation," in *Luther and the Dawn of the Modern Era,* ed. Oberman, pp. 150–157, esp. p. 155.

51. Parker, *John Calvin,* p. 153; *C.O.* 9, 892.

2: Freedom in God's Order

1. For use of these terms in Calvin, see Benjamin Charles Milner, *Calvin's Doctrine of the Church,* ch. I.

2. Comm. John, *C.O.* 47, 111; cited by Milner, p. 19.

3. Milner, pp. 7–9.

4. Milner, p. 47.

5. T. F. Torrance, *Kingdom and Church: A Study in the Theology of the Reformation,* ch. IV.

6. Milner, pp. 10, 22, 32.

7. *Inst.* I, xiv, 21.

8. Serm. I Cor., *C.O.* 49, 719–722. Cf. Serm. Gal., *C.O.* 50, 567–570.

9. *C.O.* 7, 187–190.

10. *C.O.* 7, 186–192. Passage noted in the context of providence by Wendel, *Calvin,* pp. 179–180.

11. *O.S.* III, 6. Cf. T. H. L. Parker, *Calvin's New Testament Commentaries,* pp. 1–10, 53–54.

12. *Inst.* I, v, 1.

13. *Inst.* I, v, 1–3.

14. *Inst.* I, xiv, 20. Cf. *Inst.* I, xvi, 7.

15. *Inst.* I, xiv, 20–21.

16. *Inst.* II, ii, 16. Cf. *Inst.* I, xvi, 1–3, 4, 7, 9.

17. *Inst.* II, ii, 17.

18. *Inst.* II, viii, 41–43.

19. *Inst.* II, viii, 36.

20. Serm. I Tim., *C.O.* 53, 209–222.

21. Comm. Gen., *C.O.* 23, 27, 29.

92. Comm. Gen., *C.O.* 23, 28; cf. 55, 68.

23. Serm. Eph., *C.O.* 51, 798.

24. Comm. Gen., *C.O.* 23, 44. Adam "played" and took delight in work before the Fall. Comm. Gen., *C.O.* 23, 73.

25. Comm. Gen., *C.O.* 23, 50. On polygamy see Serm. I Tim., *C.O.* 53, 245–246.

26. Comm. Gen., *C.O.* 23, 32.

27. Comm. Gen., *C.O.* 23, 75.

28. *Inst.* II, viii, 35–36; Comm. Deut., *C.O.* 26, 310; cited by Ronald Wallace, *Calvin's Doctrine of the Christian Life,* p. 158; cf. p. 159. Cf. Torrance, *Kingdom and Church,* p. 44. Cf. Comm. I Pet., *C.O.* 55, 243–249.

29. Serm. I Tim., *C.O.* 53, 245–246.

30. *Inst.* II, viii, 38; Serm. Harm. evang., *C.O.* 46, 473–475.

31. *Inst.* IV, xx, 32; Serm. Harm. evang., *C.O.* 46, 474–475.

32. Comm. I Cor., *C.O.* 49, 416–417; Comm. Eph., *C.O.* 51, 230–231.

33. *Inst.* IV, xx, 32.

34. 1536 *Inst.* 6, 2–6, *O.S.* I, 224–228. Cf. "The Necessity of Reforming the Church," in *Calvin: Theological Treatises,* trans. J. K. S. Reid, pp. 210–216; *C.O.* 6, 518–534.

35. 1536 *Inst.* 6, 14–31, *O.S.* I, 233–255.

36. 1536 *Inst.* 6, 32, *O.S.* I, 255.

37. 1536 *Inst.* 6, 32–34, *O.S.* I, 255–258.

38. 1536 *Inst.* 6, 32, 34, *O.S.* I, 255–258.

39. 1536 *Inst.* 6, 33, *O.S.* I, 256–257.

40. 1536 *Inst.* 6, 34, *O.S.* I, 258.

41. *Inst.* IV, x, 30. See *Inst.* IV, x, 27–32; III, xix, 7–16.

42. *Inst.* IV, x, 30.

43. Paul Lehmann, "The Reformers' Use of the Bible," *Theology Today* 3 (1946), pp. 328–344, esp. p. 343; Brian A. Gerrish, "Biblical Authority and the Continental Reformation," *Scottish Journal of Theology* 10 (1957), pp. 337–360.

44. Ford Lewis Battles, "God Was Accommodating Himself to Human Capacity," *Interpretation* 31 (1977), pp. 19–38.

45. Serm. I Cor., *C.O.* 49, 709–712, 714.

46. Serm. I Cor., *C.O.* 49, 714.

47. Serm. I Cor., *C.O.* 49, 725.

48. *Ibid.*

49. Serm. I Cor., *C.O.* 49, 715–716.

50. Serm. I Cor., *C.O.* 49, 713–714.

51. Comm. I Cor., *C.O.* 49, 475.

52. Serm. I Cor., *C.O.* 49, 743–746. Cf. Comm. I Cor., *C.O.* 49, 475.

53. Serm. I Cor., *C.O.* 49, 716–718.

54. Comm. I Cor., *C.O.* 49, 474–475; Serm. I Cor., *C.O.* 49, 718–720, 726–729. Cf. Serm. Gal., *C.O.* 50, 567–568.

55. Serm. I Cor., *C.O.* 49, 727–729; Comm. I Pet., *C.O.* 55, 247–248; Comm. I Cor., *C.O.* 49, 546–547.

56. Serm. I Cor., *C.O.* 49, 737. Cf. Comm. Col., *C.O.* 52, 126.

57. Serm. I Cor., *C.O.* 49, 721, 731.

58. Serm. I Cor., *C.O.* 49, 719–720, 730, 737–742.

59. Cf. Serm. Eph., *C.O.* 51, 737–746. This characteristic has also been noted by Wallace, pp. 148–169; André Biéler, *L'homme et la femme dans la morale calviniste*, pp. 44–52.

60. Serm. I Cor., *C.O.* 49, 730.

61. Serm. I Cor., *C.O.* 49, 719–720. Cf. Serm. Gal., *C.O.* 50, 567–568.

62. Serm. I Cor., *C.O.* 49, 722.

63. Serm. I Cor., *C.O.* 49, 728.

64. Comm. Gen., *C.O.* 23, 32.

65. *Inst.* II, viii, 31–34. Bucer, *O.S.* III, 372, 374 in notes; Augsburg Confession, art. 28. Augustine, Epist. 75, 82 (Migne, *P.L.* 33, 251ff., 275ff.); cited by Street, p. 93.

66. A. Passerin d'Entrèves, *Natural Law: An Introduction to Legal Philosophy*, p. 66.

67. D'Entrèves, p. 69.

68. D'Entrèves, pp. 69–70. Cited by David Little, *Religion, Order, and Law: A Study in Pre-Revolutionary England*, p. 41 n. 43. Though Little builds strongly on the voluntarist element in Calvin's thought, he sees little reason to connect that with nominalism. Little's ch. 3, "The New Order of John Calvin," stresses the importance of freedom and change in that order.

69. See above, chapter 1, note 42.

70. Serm. Deut., *C.O.* 26, 596. Cf. Comm. Gen., *C.O.* 23, 20, concerning God's use of the sun and moon.

71. Serm. Deut., *C.O.* 26, 597; cf. 593–597. The passage is noted by Wallace, p. 147 n. 2, but Wallace sees in it only a parallel to the Lord's Supper. Cf. Comm. Ezek., *C.O.* 40, 116; cited by Milner, p. 18.

72. See William J. Courtenay, "Covenant and Causality in Pierre d'Ailly," *Speculum* 46 (1971), pp. 94–119.

73. Serm. Harm. evang., *C.O.* 46, 541. Cf. *Inst.* IV, ii, 3.

74. Serm. Harm. evang., *C.O.* 46, 541. Passage noted by Wallace in another context, p. 143 n. 3.

75. Serm. Harm. evang., *C.O.* 46, 542.

76. *Inst.* IV, xvi, 19.

77. William J. Bouwsma, "The Two Faces of Humanism," pp. 26–28.

78. Ibid., pp. 3–60, esp. p. 49. Raymond K. Anderson, *Love and Order: The Life-structuring Dynamics of Grace and Virtue in Calvin's Ethical Thought: An Interpretation*, also stresses Calvin's place in the context of humanist transformation of classical virtue. He reevaluates the older view held by Wallace of Calvin's use of the Stoic tradition of antiquity in relation especially to "moderation" and "order" (pp. 15–17, 319–341). Bernd Moeller, *Imperial Cities and the Reformation*, also discusses a new social activism in sixteenth-century humanism (pp. 21–35). Little, on the other

hand, equates humanism with stoicism and sets Calvin over against it (pp. 36–37, 40).

79. Bouwsma, "The Two Faces of Humanism," p. 50.

80. Lucien Joseph Richard, *The Spirituality of John Calvin*, p. 175; cf. pp. 111ff. on the concept of order and the spiritual life.

81. John T. McNeill and James Hastings Nichols, *Ecumenical Testimony*, pp. 13–26; John T. McNeill, "Calvin as an Ecumenical Churchman," *Church History* 32 (1963), pp. 379–391; W. Nijenhuis, *Calvinus Oecumenicus*.

82. Comm. I Cor., *C.O.* 49, 472–473. Cf. Comm. I Cor., *C.O.* 49, 533–534.

83. *Inst.* IV, iii, 8–16; cf. Comm. Rom., *C.O.* 49, 238.

84. *Inst.* IV, iv, 2; 1536 *Inst.* 5, 60, *O.S.* I, 229.

85. Eugene Heideman, *Reformed Bishops and Catholic Elders*, pp. 113–114.

86. John Leith, *Introduction to the Reformed Tradition*, p. 139. See Catechism, *O.S.* II, 72.

87. *Inst.* IV, i, 9–12; IV, vi, 2; IV, x, 32.

88. Comm. Rom., *C.O.* 49, 238; cf. 497–498.

3: Women's Freedom in Church Order: Calvin's View

1. August Bebel, *Woman and Socialism*, trans. M. Stern, p. 62.

2. Georgia Harkness, *John Calvin: The Man and His Ethics*, p. 155.

3. Biéler, *L'homme et la femme*, p. 76.

4. Biéler, pp. 148–149.

5. John Bratt, "The Role and Status of Women in the Writings of John Calvin" in *Renaissance, Reformation, Resurgence*, ed. Peter DeKlerk, p. 1.

6. Bratt, p. 9.

7. Bratt, pp. 10–11.

8. Willis P. DeBoer, "Calvin on the Role of Women," in *Exploring the Heritage of John Calvin*, ed. David E. Holwerda, p. 236. The judgment is broadened to "the whole of his writing" (p. 256).

9. DeBoer, p. 268.

10. DeBoer, pp. 241ff., 257ff., 271–272.

11. Rita Mancha, "The Woman's Authority: Calvin to Edwards," *The Journal of Christian Reconstruction* 6 (1979/80), pp. 86–98.

12. H. Jackson Forstman, *Word and Spirit: Calvin's Doctrine of Biblical Authority*, pp. 110–111, 123.

13. DeBoer, pp. 258ff.

14. 1536 *Inst.*, *O.S.* I, 38.

15. 1536 *Inst.*, *O.S.* I, 49, 50–51.

16. 1536 *Inst.*, *O.S.* I, 53.

17. 1536 *Inst.*, *O.S.* I, 220–223.

18. 1536 *Inst.*, *O.S.* I, 77, 136, 140, 175, 178, 180, 198, 207, 218, 255.

19. 1536 *Inst.*, *O.S.* I, 208.

20. 1536 *Inst.*, *O.S.* I, 249; *aniles* becomes *inanes* after 1539.

21. 1536 *Inst. O.S.* I, 256–257. See above, chapter 2, pp. 30–31.

22. *Inst.* I, xv and II, i, 3–4; the disobedience of "one man" in Rom. 5:19 is understood here as *homo*, a human person, not a male person.

23. *Inst.* II, i, 4.

24. *Inst.* I, xv, 4.

25. *Inst.* I, xiv, 14. Cf. *Inst.* III, iv, 37.

26. *Inst.* II, x, 11, 12; II, xi, 9; III, ii, 31.

27. *Inst.* II, xiii, 1, 3; II, xvi, 5, 14.

28. *Inst.* IV, iii, 9; IV, xiii, 18–19. Both sections were added in 1543. Cf. Comm. Rom., *C.O.* 49, 240; Comm. I Tim., *C.O.* 52, 309–314.

29. *Inst.* IV, iii, 9.

30. French editions, 1545ff.

31. It is puzzling that he understands the women in 1 Tim. 3:11 to be simply the wives of deacons; see Serm. I Tim., *C.O.* 53, 302; Comm. I Tim., *C.O.* 52, 286.

32. *Inst.* IV, xiii, 18: "sui iuris et iugo maritali solutae" and "estans en liberté, et non liées par mariage."

33. *Inst.* IV, xiii, 18.

34. *Inst.* IV, xiii, 19.

35. Serm. I Cor., *C.O.* 49, 724, 730; Comm. I Cor., *C.O.* 49, 476–477.

36. *Inst.* IV, xv, 20–22. Further revised in 1545 and 1559. Cf. Appendix ad interim, *C.O.* 7, 681–686; Epist., *C.O.* 11, 625, 706. See Roger Gryson, *Le ministère des femmes dans l'église ancienne*, pp. 29–31.

37. *Inst.* IV, xvi, 8. Section added 1539. Bucer also makes this same point in a debate with an Anabaptist in Marburg, 1538. The text has been translated in Franklin H. Littell, "New Light on Butzer's Significance," in *Reformation Studies: Essays in Honor of Roland H. Bainton*, ed. F. H. Littell, p. 158. The same argument has been noted in Zwingli by Bernard J. Verkamp, *The Indifferent Mean: Adiaphorism in the English Reformation to 1554*, p. 64, citing *Von dem touff*, *S.W.* 4, 296–297.

38. *Inst.* II, xiii, 3.

39. Ibid.

40. Ibid.

41. *Inst.* II, viii, 35–38.

42. *Inst.* II, viii, 41–44.

43. *Inst.* IV, xii, 25.

44. 1536 *Inst.*, *O.S.* I, 244.

45. *Inst.* IV, viii, 13. Men and women must both learn in subjection in the church; see Serm. I Tim., *C.O.* 53, 207.

46. *Inst.* IV, x, 27–32.

47. *Inst.* IV, i, 12.

48. Parker, *Calvin's New Testament Commentaries*, p. 25.

49. Comm. I Cor., *C.O.* 49, 472–475.

50. See above, chapter 2, pp. 34–35.

51. Serm. I Cor., *C.O.* 49, 727; cf. Thomas F. Torrance, *Calvin's Doctrine of Man*, pp. 43–44.

52. Serm. I Cor., *C.O.* 49, 727.

53. Comm. I Cor., *C.O.* 49, 475–476.
54. Comm. I Cor., *C.O.* 49, 532–533.
55. Comm. I Cor., *C.O.* 49, 533.
56. Ibid.
57. Ibid.
58. Comm. I Cor., *C.O.* 49, 534.
59. Comm. I Cor., *C.O.* 49, 535.
60. Comm. I Cor., *C.O.* 49, 535–536. Cf. *Inst.* IV, x, 30.
61. Comm. Acts, *C.O.* 48, 15–16.
62. Comm. Acts, *C.O.* 48, 437–438. The Torrance translation (Acts II, p. 145) ends: ". . . so that she might not destroy the order prescribed by God and by nature," losing Calvin's nuance. Cf. Comm. Col., *C.O.* 52, 124 on mutual teaching by men and women.
63. Comm. Rom., *C.O.* 49, 285.
64. Comm. Rom., *C.O.* 49, 284–285; cf. 240.
65. Comm. Acts, *C.O.* 48, 477–478.
66. Serm. I Tim., *C.O.* 53, 221–222; Comm. I Tim., *C.O.* 52, 276.
67. Serm. I Tim., *C.O.* 53, 223. Cf. Calvin's discussion of the prophetess Anna, Comm. Harm. evang., *C.O.* 45, 95–96.
68. Serm. I Tim., *C.O.* 53, 223–224; Comm. I Tim., *C.O.* 52, 276.
69. Serm. I Tim., *C.O.* 53, 224.
70. Serm. I Tim., *C.O.* 53, 224–226; Comm. I Tim., *C.O.* 52, 277–278.
71. Serm. I Tim., *C.O.* 53, 227–229; Comm. I Tim., *C.O.* 52, 276; Serm. Deut., *C.O.* 26, 444.
72. Serm. I Tim., *C.O.* 53, 229–230.
73. Serm. I Tim., *C.O.* 53, 232.
74. Comm. I Tim., *C.O.* 52, 276–277.
75. Comm. I Tim., *C.O.* 52, 276.
76. Comm. I Tim., *C.O.* 52, 277.
77. Serm. de la passion, *C.O.* 46, 929, 931.
78. Serm. de la passion, *C.O.* 46, 943–944.
79. Comm. Harm. evang., *C.O.* 45, 792; cf. 796. For patristic references to women as apostles, see Karl Hermann Schelkle, *Der Geist und die Braut: Die Frau in der Bibel,* pp. 151–152. Prof. Bernadette Brooten called this to my attention.
80. Comm. Harm. evang., *C.O.* 45, 792–793.
81. Comm. Harm. evang., *C.O.* 45, 799.
82. Comm. John, *C.O.* 47, 432.
83. Comm. John, *C.O.* 47, 433–434.
84. Comm. John, *C.O.* 47, 434.
85. Comm. John, *C.O.* 47, 92.
86. Ibid.
87. Comm. Gen., *C.O.* 23, 28.
88. Ibid.
89. Comm. Gen., *C.O.* 23, 27.
90. Comm. Gen., *C.O.* 23, 44.

91. Comm. Gen., *C.O.* 23, 46.
92. Comm. Gen., *C.O.* 23, 46–47.
93. Comm. Gen., *C.O.* 23, 47, on Gen. 2:18; the word used is *aequabile*.
94. Comm. Gen., *C.O.* 23, 56–58.
95. Comm. Gen., *C.O.* 23, 60; see the discussion here of Paul.
96. Comm. Gen., *C.O.* 23, 47.
97. Comm. Gen., *C.O.* 23, 72.
98. Serm. Job, *C.O.* 33, 139–146.
99. Serm. Job, *C.O.* 33, 146.
100. Serm. Job, *C.O.* 33, 148.
101. Comm. I Cor., *C.O.* 49, 403.
102. Biéler, *L'homme et la femme*, p. 73; cf. pp. 73–75; on Genevan legislation, see Biéler, ch. IV. Cf. Jane D. Douglass, "Women and the Continental Reformation" in *Religion and Sexism*, ed. Rosemary R. Ruether, pp. 303–304. See below, chapter 5, note 15.
103. For example, *Inst.* II, viii, 16, 18.
104. See above, chapter 2, p. 32.
105. See above, chapter 2, pp. 33–34.
106. See below, chapter 5, pp. 94–97.

4: The Medieval and Renaissance Context

1. Natalie Zemon Davis, "Women in the Crafts in Sixteenth-Century Lyon," *Feminist Studies* 8 (1982), pp. 47–80; Davis, *Society and Culture in Early Modern France*, ch. 3.
2. Ruth Kelso, *Doctrine for the Lady of the Renaissance*.
3. Joan Kelly-Gadol, "Did Women Have a Renaissance?" in *Becoming Visible: Women in European History*, ed. Renate Bridenthal and Claudia Koonz, pp. 137–164.
4. Nancy L. Roelker, *Queen of Navarre: Jeanne d'Albret 1528–1572;* and "The Appeal of Calvinism to French Noblewomen in the Sixteenth Century," *Journal of Interdisciplinary History* 2 (1972), pp. 391–418; Gordon Griffiths, "Louise of Savoy and Reform of the Church," *Sixteenth Century Journal* 10 (1979), pp. 29–36; Myra Dickman Orth, "Francis DuMoulin and the *Journal* of Louise of Savoy," *Sixteenth Century Journal* 13 (1982), pp. 55–66.
5. Roelker, "The Appeal of Calvinism," p. 399; Roland Bainton, *Women of the Reformation in Germany and Italy*, pp. 235–251.
6. Roelker, "The Appeal of Calvinism," pp. 402–403.
7. A. Chagny and F. Girard, *Une princesse de la renaissance: Marguerite d'Autriche-Bourgogne, fondatrice de l'Église de Brou, 1480–1530*, p. 5. Cf. Biéler's list of remarkable women in *L'homme et la femme*, p. 33.
8. H. C. Eric Midelfort, *Witch Hunting in Southwestern Germany 1562–1684: The Social and Intellectual Foundations*, pp. 184–185.
9. Kelso, pp. 5–6.

10. Jeffrey Burton Russell, *Witchcraft in the Middle Ages*, esp. pp. 279–285; Midelfort, *Witch Hunting*, pp. 1–2, 182–186, 195–196; E. William Monter, "Pedestal and Stake: Courtly Love and Witchcraft" in *Becoming Visible: Women in European History*, ed. Bridenthal and Koonz, pp. 129–135.

11. Émile Telle, *L'oeuvre de Marguerite d'Angoulême, reine de Navarre, et la querelle des femmes*, chs. 1, 2, esp. p. 43. Cf. Kelso, ch. II.

12. Henricus Cornelius Agrippa von Nettesheim, "Declamatio de nobilitate et praecellentia foeminei sexus," *Opera* II, 504, 508.

13. Agrippa, *Opera* II, 505.

14. Agrippa, *Opera* II, 507. Cf. Marguerite of Valois, cited by Biéler, *L'homme et la femme*, p. 80, also by Blaisdell, "Response to John H. Bratt," in *Renaissance, Reformation, Response*, ed. DeKlerk, p. 20. Blaisdell refers to this argument that woman is superior because she was created after man in time as "frivolous" when she discusses Marguerite. But she contrasts this with Agrippa's "serious" treatise on the nobility of women. We see that Agrippa uses the same argument.

15. Agrippa, *Opera* II, 517–518.

16. Agrippa, *Opera* II, 518. The reference is to canon law, pars II, causa 33, quaestio 5, c. 13; cf. *Corpus iuris canonici*, ed. Aemilius Friedberg, I, col. 1254. The canon draws upon 1 Cor. 11.

17. Agrippa, *Opera* II, 518–519.

18. Agrippa, *Opera* II, 533–534. The mention of preaching has been noted by Telle, p. 51. Cf. Bercher, quoted by William H. Woodward, *Studies in Education During the Age of the Renaissance, 1400–1600*, p. 265.

19. Agrippa, *Opera* II, 521. Cf. Calvin, "De scandalis," *O.S.* II, 201; Telle, pp. 49, 53–54 n. 19, on possible relation to Erasmus. The reference by Telle to Ecclesiastes 13:14 should be Ecclesiasticus 42:14. My former colleague, Prof. William Brownlee of Claremont Graduate School, has shown in an unpublished manuscript that the Hebrew text on which this translation is based is corrupt and should probably be read: "Better a man's injury than a woman's rumor."

20. Henri Naef, *Les origines de la Réforme à Genève*, I, pp. 309–342.

21. Charles G. Nauert, Jr., *Agrippa and the Crisis of Renaissance Thought*, esp. ch. 7. Cf. Josef Bohatec, *Budé und Calvin: Studien zur Gedankenwelt des französischen Frühhumanismus*, pp. 162–165.

22. Comm. I Pet., *C.O.* 55, 230.

23. See above, chapter 3, p. 57.

24. See below, chapter 5, pp. 93–94.

25. Roland Bainton, *Women of the Reformation in France and England*, pp. 13–41.

26. Ibid., pp. 21, 25–28.

27. Marguerite d'Angoulême, *The Mirror of the Sinful Soul*, ed. Percy W. Ames (a facsimile edition).

28. Jules Gelernt, review of *Marguerite de Navarre: Chansons spirituelles*, ed. Georges Dottin, in *Renaissance Quarterly* 25 (1972), pp. 464–467.

29. Telle, pp. 360–363.

30. Quoted by Telle, p. 362 n. 10; see p. 363.

31. Quoted by Telle, pp. 363–364, from Story 67. Cf. *Inst.* IV, i, 6.

32. Christine de Pizan (sometimes spelled Pisan), *The Book of the City of Ladies,* trans. Earl Jeffrey Richards; see Introduction, pp. xix–li. Cf. Joan Kelly, "Early Feminist Theory and the *Querelle des Femmes,* 1400–1789," *Signs* 8 (1982), pp. 4–28.

33. Telle, pp. 63–68.

34. Ian Maclean, *The Renaissance Notion of Woman: A Study in the Fortunes of Scholasticism and Medical Science in European Intellectual Life,* p. 22.

35. Bohatec, pp. 215 n. 5, 320.

36. Sherrin Marshall Wyntjes, "Women in the Reformation Era," in *Becoming Visible: Women in European History,* ed. Bridenthal and Koonz, p. 170. Cf. J. K. Sowards, "Erasmus and the Education of Women," *Sixteenth Century Journal* 13 (1982), pp. 77–89.

37. See also Woodward, *Studies in Education During the Age of the Renaissance,* pp. 124, 204, 205, 207–209, 264, 265, 270.

38. Manfred P. Fleisher, " 'Are Women Human?'—The Debate of 1595 Between Valens Acidalius and Simon Gediccus," *Sixteenth Century Journal* 12 (1981), pp. 107–108. Socinians were the followers of Fausto Sozzini (d. 1604), active in Poland in the last decades of the century.

39. Maclean, pp. 12–13.

40. Fleischer, p. 108.

41. Maclean, pp. 12–13.

42. Fleischer, pp. 108–109.

43. Fleischer, pp. 114–120.

44. Fleischer, p. 118.

45. Karl Joseph von Hefele, *Histoire des conciles,* trans. Dom H. Leclercq, III, pt. 1, pp. 212–213 n. 7.

46. Bebel, p. 62.

47. Hefele, p. 212, n. 7.

48. Gregory of Tours, *The History of the Franks,* Book VIII, ch. 20, trans. L. Thorpe, p. 452. (Translation slightly altered.) Cf. Gregory of Tours, *Historia francorum,* Migne, *P.L.* 71, 462.

49. Hefele, pp. 213–214 n. 7.

50. Kari Elisabeth Børresen, *Subordination and Equivalence: The Nature and Role of Woman in Augustine and Thomas Aquinas,* trans. Charles H. Talbot, pp. 15–22.

51. Børresen, pp. 25–30.

52. *De trinitate* XII, 7; C.C. 50, 363–364. Quoted by Børresen, pp. 27–28.

53. Børresen, pp. 81–87.

54. Børresen, pp. 97–104.

55. Børresen, pp. 127–133.

56. Børresen, pp. 86–87.

57. Børresen, pp. 147–171, 244, 248–250, 333–334.

58. Børresen, pp. 153–156.

59. *S.T.* I, 92, 1, ad 1. Quoted by Børresen, p. 159. Cf. Maclean, pp. 8–9.

60. *S.T.* I, 93, 4, ad 1. Quoted by Børresen, p. 167.
61. Børresen, p. 168.
62. Børresen, pp. 165–168.
63. Børresen, pp. 259–271.
64. Børresen, pp. 177, 236–243.
65. Børresen, pp. 245–246.
66. *S.T.* I, 92, 1, ad 2. Quoted by Børresen, p. 171.
67. Maclean, pp. 11–14.
68. Maclean, pp. 14–15.
69. Maclean, p. 15.
70. See above, chapter 3, p. 49.
71. Maclean, pp. 28–46.
72. Maclean, pp. 35–37.
73. Menno Simons, "Reply to Gellius Faber," in Joyce Irwin, *Womanhood in Radical Protestantism: 1525–1675*, pp. 12–20.
74. Irwin, pp. 3–7, 12.
75. *Inst.* I, v, 2.
76. Børresen, p. 42.
77. *S.T.*, Supplementum 39, art. 1. Discussed by Børresen, pp. 236–237.
78. *Inst.* II, viii, 41–43.
79. Bratt, p. 13 n. 12, and DeBoer, pp. 236–237, are aware of some issues raised by the *querelle des femmes* but use that material only to stress the distance between Calvin and the Renaissance writers. Biéler, *L'homme et la femme*, pp. 33–34 and 79–81, seems more conscious of the changes taking place in sixteenth-century society and Calvin's openness to them, but he gives no examples of connection between Calvin's thought and the Renaissance world.
80. Biéler, *L'homme et la femme*, pp. 35–43, 52–63, 81–88.

5: The Reformation Context

1. Jules Le Coultre, *Maturin Cordier et les origines de la pédagogie protestante dans les pays de langue française, 1530–64*, p. 117; Naef, I, 297.
2. Luther, *An die Ratherren aller Städte deutsches Lands dass sie christliche Schulen aufrichten und halten sollen*, W.A. 15, 27–53; see also *Eine Predigt, dass man Kinder zur Schule halten solle* (1530), W.A. 30 II, 517–588; for Bucer, see *De regno christi*, II, ch. xlviii, ed. François Wendel, in *Martini Buceri Opera Latina* 15, pp. 238–240.
3. Le Coultre, p. 117.
4. Thérèse Pittard, *Femmes de Genève aux jours d'autrefois*, pp. 148–149, 151–152.
5. Irwin, p. xxi.
6. Serm. I Tim., *C.O.* 53, 254–255. Blaisdell, "Response," p. 22, seems to have misunderstood this point in claiming that Calvin holds virginity superior to marriage. See Biéler, *L'homme et la femme*, pp. 65–69.
7. Douglass, "Women and the Continental Reformation," pp. 293–296.

For a detailed study, see Steven Ozment, *When Fathers Ruled: Family Life in Reformation Europe.*

8. Miriam U. Chrisman, "Women and the Reformation in Strasbourg, 1490–1530," *ARG* 63 (1972), p. 147.

9. Ozment, *The Reformation in the Cities,* pp. 52–54.

10. Chrisman, p. 152.

11. For Calvin, see *The Register of the Company of Pastors of Geneva in the Time of Calvin,* ed. P. E. Hughes, pp. 193–198, 344–345; Epist., *C.O.* 14, 337ff.; *Consilia, C.O.* 10, 239ff.; Epist., *C.O.* 17, 539.

12. Wallace, pp. 157–169; Biéler, *L'homme et la femme,* pp. 35–64; Douglass, "Women and the Continental Reformation," pp. 301–302; F. Wendel, *Le mariage à Strasbourg à l'époque de la réforme, 1520–1692;* Chrisman, pp. 148–149; Blaisdell, "Response," p. 23; Torrance, *Calvin's Doctrine of Man,* p. 44.

13. Serm. Eph., *C.O.* 51, 735–746, esp. 740.

14. Biéler, *L'homme et la femme,* pp. 73–76; Wendel, *Le mariage à Strasbourg,* pp. 48, 146–149; Wendel, Introduction to Bucer, *De regno christi,* pp. xlix–1; Bucer, *De regno christi,* II, chs. xxii–xliv, ed. Wendel, pp. 165–226; Luther, *De captivitate babylonica,* W.A. 6, 558–559.

15. Davis, *Society and Culture,* p. 90 n.; see pp. 88–95. Cf. E. William Monter, "Women in Calvinist Geneva (1550–1800)," *Signs* 6 (1980), p. 195.

16. Bucer, *Von der Ehe,* p. 12 a, quoted and discussed by Wendel, *Le mariage à Strasbourg,* p. 46. See *De regno christi,* II, ch. xxxix, ed. Wendel, p. 209.

17. Second Helvetic Confession, XXIX, 2 (*The Creeds of Christendom,* ed. Philip Schaff, III, p. 304). There is, however, another section of ch. XXIX dealing with parents' duties. The Augsburg Confession has no corresponding emphasis on the priority of companionship in marriage. See Augsburg Conf. II, ii (in Schaff, pp. 30–34) and vi (pp. 49–58), concerning clerical celibacy; but there is no general treatment of marriage.

18. Westminster Confession, XXIV, 2, Schaff, III, p. 655.

19. Maurice Bardèche, *Histoire des femmes,* II, p. 145.

20. Bainton, *Women of the Reformation in Germany and Italy,* pp. 55–76. Cf. Chrisman, pp. 152–158. Caspar Schwenckfeld (d. 1561) was a mystic from Silesia whose followers are considered part of the "Radical Reformation."

21. Ozment, *The Reformation in the Cities,* p. 103.

22. Bard Thompson, ed., *Liturgies of the Western Church,* pp. 161–179, 101–137, 142, 147–155. See Luther, *W.A.* 26, 42, commenting on change in women's participation.

23. Thompson, pp. 185–208. Cf. Comm. Col., *C.O.* 52, 124–125; Comm. I Cor., *C.O.* 49, 522.

24. Claude Haton, *Mémoires de Claude Haton,* ed. F. Bourquelot, *Collection des documents inédits sur l'histoire de France* (Paris, 1857), 1:49–50; quoted by Davis, *Society and Culture,* p. 86.

25. "The Necessity of Reforming the Church," *C.O.* 6, 483; trans. in *Calvin: Theological Treatises,* p. 197.

26. *W.A.* 26, 47; cf. 46–49.

27. *W.A.* 26, 49.

28. *W.A.* 26, 47.

29. *W.A.* 26, 85–94. On 1 Tim. 3:11, both Calvin and Luther assume Paul is discussing the wives of deacons, not women deacons (*W.A.* 26, 61; Comm. I Tim., *C.O.* 52, 286). After completion of this chapter, I found the newly published work by Elsie Anne McKee, *John Calvin on the Diaconate and Liturgical Almsgiving.* She concludes (pp. 213ff.) that Calvin is the first Reformer to see the women deacons' ministry as a public office. She notes that for a few years at the end of the sixteenth century the office was actually revived for women in the Synod of Wesel in the Rhineland (pp. 220–221).

30. François Wendel, *L'église de Strasbourg: sa constitution et son organisation, 1532–1535,* pp. 190–192.

31. *Les lettres à Jean Calvin de la collection Sarrau,* ed. Rodolphe Peter and Jean Rott, pp. 71–75. Noted by Kingdon while still unpublished; see Robert M. Kingdon, *Geneva and the Consolidation of the French Protestant Movement 1564–1572,* p. 48.

32. Kingdon, pp. 43–137.

33. Jehan Morély, *Traicté de la discipline et police Chrestienne* (Lyon, 1562; repr. Geneva, 1968), pp. 247–248.

34. Morély, pp. 251, 254, 255.

35. Morély, pp. 255–256.

36. Kingdon, pp. 62, 59.

37. Kingdon, p. 59.

38. Morély, pp. 247, 251.

39. Morély, A 2^v.

40. Morély, A 2^v–A 3^r. This point of view is also suggested on pp. 246–247, 123.

41. Marginal notations on pp. 254 and 255 indicate Acts 6 as support. These notations may or may not be those of Morély himself. It is not clear how this chapter proves married women served in this capacity, since the deacons elected there were men. But on p. 253 he suggests women were chosen for the daily service before the institution of deacons. On p. 254 concerning election of deacons, Morély says, "De quoy nous avons exemple en la primitive Eglise: comme en ce que les femmes des Grecs murmuroyent de ce qu'elles se voyent reiettees du service quotidian. . . ." Acts 6:1 recounts that "the Hellenists murmured against the Hebrews because their widows were neglected in the daily distribution." Morély may simply be mistaken here—and trying to be consistently biblical.

42. Morély, pp. 119–120. Cited by Kingdon, p. 52.

43. We must assume they were acquainted in such a small city. Cf. James I. Good, *Women of the Reformed Church,* p. 49: "When Calvin came fleeing from France, having had all his money stolen on the way, it was Mrs. Zell who gave him a warm welcome at her fireside." No evidence is cited. Cf. Bainton, *Women of the Reformation in Germany and Italy,* p. 64. There is no

specific mention of Katherine in the letter cited by Bainton recounting a visit to the Zell house (*C.O.* 10, 398).

44. Bainton, *Women of the Reformation in Germany and Italy*, p. 55.

45. *W.A.* 13, 110.

46. *W.A.* 13, 111.

47. Comm. Joel, *C.O.* 42, 564–570.

48. Comm. Acts, *C.O.* 48, 31–32.

49. Davis, *Society and Culture,* p. 83. Morély approves such lay prophesying; see Kingdon, pp. 106–109, cited by Davis. But Kingdon makes no specific mention of women taking part, and in view of our discussion above, it does not seem likely that Morély would include them.

50. Calvin A. Pater, *Karlstadt as the Father of the Baptist Movements,* p. 72; cf. pp. 66–73. On p. 309 he cites an edition by Melchior Hoffman of visions of the Strasbourg prophetess Ursula Jost.

51. Roland Bainton, *Women of the Reformation in Germany and Italy; Women of the Reformation in France and England; Women of the Reformation from Spain to Scandinavia.*

52. Quoted by Richard L. Greaves, *Theology and Revolution in the Scottish Reformation: Studies in the Thought of John Knox,* p. 158.

53. Greaves, pp. 157–168.

54. *The First Blast of the Trumpet Against the Monstrous Regiment of Women* (1558), in *The Works of John Knox,* ed. David Laing, vol. IV, pp. 366–373.

55. Knox, p. 374.

56. Knox, p. 375.

57. Knox, pp. 377–400, 420.

58. Greaves, pp. 160–161.

59. Greaves, pp. 163–168. Wyntjes, p. 178, simply says he recanted.

60. Epist., *C.O.* 15, 91–92, 125, correspondence between Calvin and Bullinger.

61. Greaves, p. 159. Comm. Isa., *C.O.* 36 Prolegomena; Epist., *C.O.* 17, 490–492.

62. Epist., *C.O.* 15, 125. Cf. Epist., *C.O.* 15, 92 for the Zurich statement.

63. Epist., *C.O.* 17, 490–492. Women's ruling is not discussed in the commentary on Isa. 3:12; see Comm. Isa., *C.O.* 36, 88.

64. Bainton, *Women of the Reformation in Germany and Italy,* pp. 97–100.

65. See Roelker, "The Appeal of Calvinism," and Charmarie Jenkins Blaisdell, "Calvin's Letters to Women: The Courting of Ladies in High Places," *Sixteenth Century Journal* 13 (1982), pp. 67–84.

66. Cf. Roelker, "The Role of Noblewomen in the French Reformation," *ARG* 63 (1972), pp. 168–195; Good, *Women of the Reformed Church;* Bainton, *Women of the Reformation in France and England.*

67. Kingdon, p. 97. Davis adds that she had no vote; see *Society and Culture,* p. 84 n. 45.

68. Blaisdell, "Response," p. 26. Cf. Blaisdell, "Calvin's Letters to Women," p. 83; Epist., *C.O.* 20, 208, 266–273; Blaisdell, "Renée de France

Between Reform and Counter-Reform," *ARG* 63 (1972), pp. 196–226.

69. Wyntjes, pp. 179–181. It is interesting that only three women, all French or Dutch, are identifiable among the many names of leaders commemorated in decorations at the Second Council of the Alliance of the Reformed Churches holding the Presbyterian System in Philadelphia in 1880: Margaret of Valois (undoubtedly the one we have been calling Marguerite of Angoulême, Queen of Navarre, since the woman more commonly known as Margaret of Valois, wife of Henry of Navarre, was Catholic and no heroine of the French Reformed Church) and Jeanne d'Albret, her daughter and later alsŏ Queen of Navarre, on the French column, and Juliana of Stolberg, mother of William of Orange, on the column representing Holland, all noblewomen involved in political life. Henry Christopher McCook, *Historic Decorations at the Pan-Presbyterian Council: A Photographic Souvenir*, pp. 21, 31.

70. Chrisman, p. 143. But see Bainton's warning, "Introduction," *ARG* 63 (1972), p. 141. Cf. Roelker, "The Appeal of Calvinism," pp. 391ff.

71. *W.A.* 20, 148–149. Unfortunately we have no systematic work parallel to the *Institutes* from Luther to aid us in placing comments such as these in context. Without a careful and thorough monograph on the topic, we should be cautious about generalizing from a few quotations.

72. Jeanne de Jussie, *Le levain du calvinisme, ou commencement de l'hérésie de Genève* (Chambéry, 1661; repr. Geneva, 1853), pp. 164, 167.

73. Naef, I, 297–299.

74. Jussie, p. 106. For the opposite view from a contemporary Catholic man, see Davis, *Society and Culture*, p. 65.

75. Jussie, pp. 33–35.

76. Jussie, pp. 88–89. Undoubtedly the reference is to William Farel, although Sister Jeanne consistently calls him "Faret."

77. Jussie, pp. 106–109. See also Pittard, pp. 134–135, for women disciplined in the 1540s for not attending sermons or learning French prayers.

78. Jussie, pp. 146–150.

79. Jussie, pp. 54ff.

80. Jussie, pp. 54–55; cf. pp. 70–72.

81. Jussie, pp. 56–57.

82. Jussie, pp. 89–90.

83. Jussie, pp. 86–88.

84. Jussie, p. 164. The name is also spelled d'Entière.

85. Jussie, p. 165.

86. Jussie, pp. 176–177.

87. Jussie, p. 86; cf. p. 110.

88. Jussie, pp. 118–156.

89. Jussie, p. 118.

90. Jussie, p. 163.

91. Jussie, pp. 131–132.

92. Jussie, p. 134.

93. Anthoine Fromment, *Les Actes et gestes merveilleux de la cité de Genève, Nouvellement convertie à l'Evangile faictz du temps de leur Reformation et comment ils l'ont receue redigez par escript en fourme de Chroniques Annales ou Hystoyres commençant l'an MDXXXII*, ed. Gustave Revilloid, pp. 4, 5, 11, 17.

94. Fromment, pp. 45–46.

95. Fromment, pp. 15–21.

96. Fromment, pp. 17–18.

97. Fromment, pp. 18–20.

98. Fromment, p. 44. See Jussie, p. 44. Fromment tells of one Protestant woman who took up the sword enthusiastically to defend her family in a battle outside the city (p. 195).

99. Fromment, p. 224.

100. Fromment, p. 233.

101. Davis, *Society and Culture*, p. 83n.

102. Marie Dentière, *La guerre et deslivrance de la ville de Genesve* (1536), in A. Rilliet, ed., *Mémoires et documents publiés par la Société d'histoire et d'archéologie de Genève*, 20 (1881), p. 312. Introduction and text, pp. 309–376. An appendix includes "Défense pour les Femmes" and extracts from the "Epistre très utile," pp. 377–384.

103. Dentière in Rilliet, pp. 339–343. Cf. Dentière in *Correspondance des réformateurs dans les pays de langue française*, ed. A.–L. Herminjard (Geneva, 1874), V, p. 300.

104. Dentière, "Epistre très utile," in Herminjard, V, pp. 295–304. The covering letter is printed here in its entirety, along with extracts from the "Epistre très utile." See Rilliet, pp. 377–378. Some selections from the writings of Dentière translated by Thomas Head will be included in *Renaissance Women Writers*, ed. Katharina Wilson, forthcoming from University of Georgia Press.

105. Herminjard, V, p. 295, n. 2; cf. Rilliet, pp. 319–335.

106. Herminjard, V, p. 296, n. 2; pp. 302–303, n. 18; Davis, *Society and Culture*, pp. 82, 85.

107. Dentière, in Herminjard, V, pp. 297–298.

108. Dentière, in Rilliet, pp. 378–380.

109. See above, chapter 3, p. 59. For Katherine Zell's use of this imagery, see Bainton, *Women of the Reformation in Germany and Italy*, pp. 66–67.

110. Dentière, in Rilliet, p. 380. Davis, *Society and Culture*, also partially quotes this passage, p. 85.

111. Comm. I Cor., *C.O.* 49, 532–533. See above, p. 52.

112. Monter, "Women in Calvinist Geneva," p. 196; cf. pp. 189–199. See Monter, *Witchcraft in France and Switzerland: The Borderlands During the Reformation*, esp. chs. 1 and 2 and Appendix 1.

113. Monter, "Women in Calvinist Geneva," pp. 204–207.

114. See Augsburg Confession I, xv; II, v (art. xxvi); II, vii (art. xxviii); Tetrapolitan Confession, 1530, XIV; Geneva Confession, 1536, XVII; French Confession, 1559, XXXIII; Second Helvetic Confession, 1566, XXVII; Belgic Confession, 1561, XXXII.

115. See Augsburg Conf. I, xv; II, v (art. xxvi); II, vii (art. xxviii); Tetrapolitan Conf. XIV; Geneva Conf., 1536, XVII; French Conf., 1559, XXXIII; Second Helvetic Conf. XXVII; Belgic Conf., 1561, XXXII; Thirty-nine Articles, art. XXXIV.
116. W. Nijenhuis, "Calvin and the Augsburg Confession," in *Ecclesia Reformata: Studies on the Reformation*, pp. 97–114.
117. See Augsburg Conf. II, vii (art. xxviii); Geneva Conf. XVII; Tetrapolitan Conf. XIV, trans. A. Cochrane, *Reformed Confessions of the 16th Century*, p. 72. The Geneva Confession statement is less similar to Calvin's view than the other two. For authorship see Cochrane, p. 119.
118. For the various sorts of conflicts in Geneva, see Wendel, *Calvin*, chs. 2 and 3.

6: Freedom in Obedience

1. Comm. I Pet., *C.O.* 55, 246.
2. *Inst.* II, viii, 15.
3. Serm. de la passion, *C.O.* 46, 924.
4. Roger Mehl has described the difference in similar terms: *Catholic Ethics and Protestant Ethics*, pp. 19–27.
5. Cf. *Inst.* II, vii, 6–17, esp. 12ff. See I. John Hesselink, "Christ, the Law, and the Christian: An Unexplored Aspect of the Third Use of the Law in Calvin's Theology," in *Reformatio perennis*, ed. B. A. Gerrish, pp. 11–26.
6. Comm. I Tim., *C.O.* 52, 278; Serm. I Tim. 53, 232. Cf. Serm. de la passion, *C.O.* 46, 947–948; Catechism, *O.S.* II, 111–112.
7. Salo W. Baron, "John Calvin and the Jews," *Harry Austryn Wolfson: Jubilee Volume on the Occasion of His Seventy-fifth Birthday*, ed. Saul Lieberman, I, p. 161.
8. Baron, pp. 160–161.
9. See, for example, Moeller, p. 37.
10. Bouwsma, "Renaissance and Reformation," pp. 148–149.
11. Heiko A. Oberman, "Headwaters of the Reformation," in *Luther and the Dawn of the Modern Era*, ed. Oberman, p. 52.
12. *Inst.* II, viii, 16; II, viii, 1–6. Cf. *Inst.* III, vii, 1–9.
13. Catechism, *O.S.* II, 75.
14. Catechism, *O.S.* II, 96, 111, 113, 127. Cf. *Inst.* I, xii, 2; II, viii, 5.
15. John Greenleaf Whittier, text of hymn, "O Brother Man, Fold to Thy Heart Thy Brother," *The Hymnbook* (Richmond, Va., 1955), 474.
16. Calvin's translation of the text, Serm. de la nativité de Jésus Christ, *C.O.* 46, 955.
17. Serm. nat., *C.O.* 46, 965.
18. Catechism, *O.S.* II, 76.
19. Catechism, *O.S.* II, 80.
20. Ibid.
21. Catechism, *O.S.* II, 80–81.

22. Serm. Job, *C.O.* 34, 425; cf. 342–343, 423–425. Cf. *Inst.* I, v, 8; I, xiv, 18; III, ii, 11, 15, 36; Comm. I Tim., *C.O.* 52, 287; Serm. I Tim., *C.O.* 53, 239; Serm. I Cor., *C.O.* 49, 704–705; Comm. Num., *C.O.* 25, 174; Serm. I Tim., *C.O.* 53, 302–303.

23. Bonnet, I, p. 366. Quoted by Mancha, pp. 91–92. Cf. Comm. I Tim., *C.O.* 52, 277–278; Dedicatory Epistle to *De scandalis, O.S.* II, 163.

24. Charmarie Jenkins Blaisdell, "Calvin's Letters to Women," p. 73; cf. pp. 67–84. It would now be useful to work through these letters with the results of the present study in mind, looking for further evidence.

25. Catechism, *O.S.* II, 116–117.

26. Catechism, *O.S.* II, 122. Cf. Serm. I Tim., *C.O.* 53, 238–239.

27. Catechism, *O.S.* II, 127ff.

28. Catechism, *O.S.* II, 142. Cf. *Inst.* IV, xiv, 1.

29. See Carlos M. N. Eire, "Calvin and Nicodemism: A Reappraisal," *Sixteenth Century Journal* 10 (1979), pp. 45–69.

30. Serm. de la passion, *C.O.* 46, 931.

31. Serm. Job, *C.O.* 33, 144–145; *Inst.* I, ii, 1–2; I, v, 4; IV, i, 5; Comm. Ex., *C.O.* 25, 173; Serm. Job, *C.O.* 34, 426.

32. Comm. Gen., *C.O.* 23, 27–31, 37–38. Cf. Comm. Joel, *C.O.* 42, 545; *Inst.* I, xiv, 22.

33. Comm. Gen., *C.O.* 23, 44; cf. 21.

34. *Inst.* I, xiv, 22; Wendel, *Calvin,* p. 178 n. 86.

35. *Inst.* I, xiv, 22.

36. *Inst.* II, viii, 57; cf. 53.

37. Catechism, *O.S.* II, 111–112.

38. Catechism, *O.S.* II, 110.

39. Comm. Acts, *C.O.* 48, 303. Cf. *Inst.* II, viii, 55; II, xi, 11–12; III, xx, 38.

40. *Inst.* III, xx, 38, 47.

41. Comm. Gen., *C.O.* 23, 28, 48–49; Serm. I Cor., *C.O.* 49, 737; *Inst.* II, viii, 41. Cf. Torrance, *Calvin's Doctrine of Man,* pp. 44–45; Wallace, pp. 148ff.

42. *Inst.* II, ii, 16.

43. *Inst.* III, vii, 6.

44. Torrance, *Kingdom and Church,* pp. 162–163.

45. Bouwsma, "Renaissance and Reformation," pp. 134–135, 146, 147.

46. Moeller, pp. 20–35.

47. Moeller, p. 46.

48. Moeller, pp. 61–68. For a critique of the discussion, see Thomas A. Brady, Jr., *Ruling Class, Regime and Reformation at Strasbourg, 1520–1555,* pp. 3–19; Brady, " 'Social History of the Reformation,' A Conference at the Deutsches Historisches Institut, London, May 25–27, 1978," *Sixteenth Century Journal* 10 (1979), pp. 89–92.

49. Moeller, pp. 90, 92.

50. For a survey of the social situation in Geneva, see W. Fred Graham, *The Constructive Revolutionary: John Calvin and His Socio-economic Impact.* For

Calvin's thought about social issues, see André Biéler, *La pensée économique et sociale de Calvin;* the English translation by Paul T. Fuhrmann, *The Social Humanism of Calvin,* is of a much briefer work by Biéler, though it includes some similar material.

51. Harm. evang., *C.O.* 45, 689.
52. Comm. II Cor., *C.O.* 50, 102. Cf. *Inst.* II, viii, 45.
53. *Inst.* III, vii, 1–2.
54. *Inst.* III, vii, 7; cf. 1–10.
55. Serm. I Tim., *C.O..* 53, 219–221. Cf. *Inst.* IV, xx, 6.
56. Comm. I Cor., *C.O.* 49, 468.
57. *Inst.* III, xix, 11.
58. Serm. nat., *C.O.* 46, 966–968.
59. *Inst.* II, iv, 7.
60. *Inst.* III, vii, 1. Cf. Catechism, *O.S.* II, 122.
61. *Inst.* III, xxiii, 12.
62. *Inst.* III, i, 3. Cf. Serm. Deut., *C.O.* 27, 33.
63. See Kingdon, pp. 128, 135, 137.

Bibliography

I. Writings of John Calvin

Calvin, John. *Opera quae supersunt omnia*, ed. G. Baum, E. Cunitz, E. Reuss. 59 vols.; *Corpus Reformatorum*, vols. 29–88. Brunswick and Berlin, 1863–1900. Cited as *C.O.*

———. *Opera Selecta*, ed. Peter Barth and Wilhelm Niesel. 5 vols. Munich, 1926–1962. Cited as *O.S.*

———. *Institution de la religion chrestienne* (1541), ed. A. Lefranc. Paris, 1911.

———. *Institution de la religion chrestienne*, édition critique (1560), ed. Jean-Daniel Benoit. 5 vols. Paris, 1957–1963.

References to the 1559 *Institutes* are by book, chapter, and section. Translations of Calvin's writings quoted in the text from the *Institutes* or the commentaries are based upon the following translations, though freely altered:

Institutes of the Christian Religion (1559), ed. John T. McNeill, trans. Ford Lewis Battles. 2 vols. Philadelphia: Westminster Press, 1960.

Institution of the Christian Religion (1536), trans. Ford Lewis Battles. Atlanta: John Knox Press, 1975.

Calvin's New Testament Commentaries, ed. D. W. Torrance and T. F. Torrance. Grand Rapids: Wm. B. Eerdmans Publishing Co., 1959–1972.

Calvin: Commentaries on the First Book of Moses Called Genesis, trans. J. King. 1843–1855; repr. Grand Rapids: Wm. B. Eerdmans Publishing Co., 1963.

Calvin: Theological Treatises, trans. J. K. S. Reid. Philadelphia:

Westminster Press, 1954. Includes "The Catechism of the Church of Geneva" (1545) and "The Necessity of Reforming the Church" (1539).

All other translations are by the author.

II. Other Primary Sources

Agrippa von Nettesheim, Henricus Cornelius. "Declamatio de nobilitate et praecellentia foeminei sexus." In *Opera,* vol. II, pp. 504–537. Lyon, n.d.; photo. repr. Hildesheim, 1970.

Augustine. *Opera.* Turnhout, 1958–. *Corpus Christianorum, Series Latina,* vols. 27–59. Cited as *C.C.*

Bucer, Martin. *De regno christi,* ed. François Wendel. *Martini Buceri Opera Latina,* vol. 15. Paris, 1955.

Cochrane, Arthur C., ed. *Reformed Confessions of the 16th Century.* Philadelphia: Westminster Press, 1966.

Dentière, Marie. *La guerre et deslivrance de la ville de Genesve* (1536), with excerpts from *L'Épistre très utile, including Défense pour les Femmes,* in A. Rilliet, ed., *Mémoires et documents publiés par la Société d'histoire et d'archéologie de Genève* 20 (1881), pp. 309–384. Originally attributed to "ung Marchant demourant en icelle."

———. *Epistre très utile faicte et composée par une femme Chrestienne de Tornay, Envoyée à la Royne de Navarre seur du Roy de France (1539).* In *Correspondance des réformateurs,* ed. A.-L. Herminjard, vol. V, pp. 295–304. Geneva, 1874; repr. Nieuwkoop, 1966.

Friedberg, Aemilius, ed. *Corpus iuris canonici.* Leipzig, 1879; photo. repr. Graz. 1959.

Fromment, Anthoine. *Les Actes et gestes merveilleux de la cité de Genève, Nouvellement convertie à l'Evangile faictz du temps de leur Reformation et comment ils l'ont receue redigez par escript en fourme de Chroniques Annales ou Hystoyres commençant l'an MDXXXII,* ed. Gustave Revilliod. Geneva, 1854.

Gregory of Tours. *Historia francorum.* In *Patrologia Latina,* ed. J.-P. Migne, vol. 71. Paris, 1879. Cited as *P.L.*

———. *The History of the Franks,* trans. L. Thorpe. New York, 1978.

Herminjard, A.–L., ed. *Correspondance des réformateurs dans les pays de langue française.* Geneva, 1874; repr. Nieuwkoop, 1966.

Hughes, P. E., ed. *The Register of the Company of Pastors of Geneva in the Time of Calvin.* Grand Rapids: Wm. B. Eerdmans Publishing Co., 1966.

Jussie, Jeanne de. *Le levain du calvinisme, ou commencement de l'hérésie de Genève.* Chambéry, 1661; repr. Geneva, 1853.

Knox, John. "The First Blast of the Trumpet Against the Monstrous Regiment of Women." In *The Works of John Knox,* ed. David Laing, vol. IV, pp. 366–373. Edinburgh, 1885.

Lietzmann, Hans, Heinrich Bornkamm, Hans Volz, and Ernst Wolf, eds. *Die Bekenntnisschriften der evangelisch-lutherischen Kirche.* Göttingen, 1952.

Luther, Martin. *D. Martin Luthers Werke: Kritische Gesamtausgabe.* Weimar,

1883–. Cited as *W.A.* Translations in the text are based on *Luther's Works* (St. Louis: Concordia Publishing House, 1955–), though freely altered.

Marguerite d'Angoulême, Queen of Navarre. *The Mirror of the Sinful Soul,* 1544 trans. by Princess (later Queen) Elizabeth, ed. Percy W. Ames. London, 1897, facsimile ed.

Melanchthon, Philipp. *Opera quae supersunt omnia,* ed. C. G. Bretschneider. Brunswick, 1834–1860; *Corpus Reformatorum,* vols. 1–28. Cited as *C.R.*

Morély, Jehan. *Traicté de la discipline et police Chrestienne.* Lyon, 1562; photo. repr. Geneva, 1968.

Niesel, Wilhelm, ed. *Bekenntnisschriften und Kirchenordnungen der nach Gottes Wort reformierten Kirche.* Munich, 1938.

Peter, Rodolphe, and Jean Rott, eds. *Les lettres à Jean Calvin de la collection Sarrau.* Cahiers de la Revue d'Histoire et de Philosophie religieuses 43. Paris, 1972.

Pizan, Christine de. *The Book of the City of Ladies,* trans. Earl Jeffrey Richards. New York: Persea Books, 1982.

Schaff, Philip, ed. *The Creeds of Christendom: With a History and Critical Notes.* Vol. III, *The Evangelical Protestant Creeds, with Translations.* Grand Rapids: Baker Book House, 1969.

Simons, Menno. "Reply to Gellius Faber." In Joyce Irwin, *Womanhood in Radical Protestantism: 1525–1675,* pp. 12–20. New York: Edwin Mellen Press, 1979.

Thomas Aquinas, *Summa theologiae.* Ottawa, 1953. Cited as *S.T.*

Thompson, Bard, ed. *Liturgies of the Western Church.* Cleveland: World Publishing Co., Meridian Books, 1961.

III. Secondary Sources

Anderson, Raymond Kemp. *Love and Order: The Life-structuring Dynamics of Grace and Virtue in Calvin's Ethical Thought: An Interpretation.* Chambersburg, Pa.: Anderson, 1973.

Bainton, Roland H. "The Role of Women in the Reformation: Introduction to the Following Three Papers." *Archiv für Reformationsgeschichte* 63 (1972), pp. 141–142.

———. *Women of the Reformation in Germany and Italy.* Minneapolis: Augsburg Publishing House, 1971.

———. *Women of the Reformation in France and England.* Minneapolis: Augsburg Publishing House, 1973.

———. *Women of the Reformation from Spain to Scandinavia.* Minneapolis: Augsburg Publishing House, 1977.

Bardèche, Maurice. *Histoire des femmes.* Paris, 1968.

Baron, Salo W. "John Calvin and the Jews." In *Harry Austryn Wolfson: Jubilee Volume on the Occasion of His Seventy-fifth Birthday,* ed. Saul Lieberman. Jerusalem: American Academy for Jewish Research, 1965.

Battles, Ford Lewis. *A Computerized Concordance to Institutio christianae religionis, 1559.* Pittsburgh: Pittsburgh Theological Seminary, 1972.

————. "God Was Accommodating Himself to Human Capacity." *Interpretation* 31 (1977), pp. 19–38.

Bebel, August. *Woman and Socialism*, trans. M. Stern. New York, 1910.

Biéler, André. *La pensée économique et sociale de Calvin.* Geneva, 1959.

————. *L'homme et la femme dans la morale calviniste: La doctrine réformée sur l'amour, le mariage, le célibat, le divorce, l'adultère et la prostitution, considerée dans son cadre historique.* Geneva, 1963.

————. *The Social Humanism of Calvin*, trans. Paul T. Fuhrmann. Richmond, Va.: John Knox Press, 1964.

Blaisdell, Charmarie Jenkins. "Renée de France Between Reform and Counter-Reform." *Archiv für Reformationsgeschichte* 63 (1972), pp. 196–226.

————. "Response to John H. Bratt, 'The Role and Status of Women in the Writings of John Calvin.'" In *Renaissance, Reformation, Response*, ed. Peter DeKlerk. Grand Rapids: Calvin Theological Seminary, 1976.

————. "Calvin's Letters to Women: The Courting of Ladies in High Places." *Sixteenth Century Journal* 13 (1982), pp. 67–84.

Bohatec, Josef. *Budé und Calvin. Studien zur Gedankenwelt des französischen Frühumanismus.* Graz, 1950.

Børresen, Kari Elisabeth. *Subordination and Equivalence: The Nature and Role of Woman in Augustine and Thomas Aquinas*, trans. Charles H. Talbot. Washington, D.C.: University Press of America, 1981.

Bouwsma, William J. "Renaissance and Reformation: An Essay in Their Affinities and Connections." In *Luther and the Dawn of the Modern Era*, ed. Heiko A. Oberman. Leiden: E. J. Brill, 1974.

————. "The Two Faces of Humanism, Stoicism, and Augustinianism in Renaissance Thought." In *Itinerarium Italicum: The Profile of the Italian Renaissance in the Mirror of Its European Transformations*, ed. Heiko A. Oberman and Thomas A. Brady, Jr. Leiden: E. J. Brill, 1975.

Brady, Thomas A., Jr. *Ruling Class, Regime and Reformation at Strasbourg, 1520–1555.* Leiden: E. J. Brill, 1978.

————. "'Social History of the Reformation: Sozialgeschichte der Reformation': A Conference at the Deutsches Historisches Institut, London, May 25–27, 1978." *Sixteenth Century Journal* 10 (1979), pp. 89–92.

Bratt, John H. "The Role and Status of Women in the Writings of John Calvin" (with response by Charmarie Jenkins Blaisdell). In *Renaissance, Reformation, Resurgence: Colloquium on Calvin and Calvin Studies*, ed. Peter DeKlerk, pp. 1–17. Grand Rapids: Calvin Theological Seminary, 1976.

Breen, Quirinus. *John Calvin: A Study in French Humanism.* Grand Rapids, 1931; repr. Hamden, Conn.: Shoe String Press, Archon Books, 1968.

————. "St. Thomas and Calvin as Theologians: A Comparison." In *The Heritage of John Calvin*, ed. John H. Bratt, pp. 23–39. Grand Rapids: Wm. B. Eerdmans Publishing Co., 1973.

Bridenthal, Renate, and Claudia Koonz. *Becoming Visible: Women in European History.* Boston: Houghton Mifflin Co., 1977.

Chagny, A., and F. Girard. *Une princesse de la renaissance: Marguerite d'Autriche-Bourgogne, fondatrice de l'Église de Brou, 1480–1530.* Chambéry, 1929.

Chrisman, Miriam U. "Women and the Reformation in Strasbourg, 1490–1530." *Archiv für Reformationsgeschichte* 63 (1972), pp. 141–168.

Coultre, Jules Le. *Maturin Cordier et les origines de la pédagogie protestante dans les pays de langue française, 1530–64.* Neuchâtel, 1926.

Courtenay, William J. "Covenant and Causality in Pierre d'Ailly." *Speculum* 46 (1971), pp. 94–119.

Davis, Natalie Zemon. *Society and Culture in Early Modern France.* Stanford: Stanford University Press, 1975.

————. "Women in the Crafts in Sixteenth-Century Lyon." *Feminist Studies* 8 (1982), pp. 47–80.

DeBoer, Willis P. "Calvin on the Role of Women." In *Exploring the Heritage of John Calvin: Essays in Honor of John H. Bratt,* ed. D. E. Holwerda, pp. 236–272. Grand Rapids: Baker Book House, 1976.

Douglass, E. Jane Dempsey. *Justification in Late Medieval Preaching: A Study of John Geiler of Keisersberg.* Leiden: E. J. Brill, 1966.

————. "Women and the Continental Reformation." In *Religion and Sexism: Images of Woman in the Jewish and Christian Traditions,* ed. Rosemary R. Ruether, pp. 292–318. New York: Simon & Schuster, 1974.

Eire, Carlos M. N. "Calvin and Nicodemism: A Reappraisal," *Sixteenth Century Journal* 10 (1979), pp. 45–69.

Entrèves, Allessandro Passerin d'. *Natural Law: An Introduction to Legal Philosophy.* London: Hutchinson, 1967.

Feinberg, John Samuel. "The Doctrine of Human Freedom in the Writings of John Calvin." M.Th. thesis, Trinity Evangelical Divinity School, Deerfield, Ill., 1972.

Fleischer, Manfred P. " 'Are Women Human?'—The Debate of 1595 Between Valens Acidalius and Simon Gediccus." *Sixteenth Century Journal* 12 (1981), pp. 107–120.

Forstman, H. Jackson. *Word and Spirit: Calvin's Doctrine of Biblical Authority.* Stanford: Stanford University Press, 1962.

Ganoczy, Alexandre. *Le Jeune Calvin: Genèse et évolution de sa vocation réformatrice.* Wiesbaden: Franz Steiner Verlag, 1966.

Gelernt, Jules. Review of *Marguerite de Navarre: Chansons spirituelles,* ed. Georges Dottin (Geneva, 1971). In *Renaissance Quarterly* 25 (1972), pp. 464–467.

Gerrish, Brian A. "Biblical Authority and the Continental Reformation." *Scottish Journal of Theology* 10 (1957), pp. 337–360.

Good, James I. *Women of the Reformed Church.* Sunday-School Board of the Reformed Church in the United States, 1901.

Graham, W. Fred. *The Constructive Revolutionary: John Calvin and His Socio-economic Impact.* Richmond, Va.: John Knox Press, 1971.

Greaves, Richard L. *Theology and Revolution in the Scottish Reformation: Studies in the Thought of John Knox.* Grand Rapids: Wm. B. Eerdmans Publishing Co., 1980.

Griffiths, Gordon. "Louise of Savoy and Reform of the Church." *Sixteenth Century Journal* 10 (1979), pp. 29–36.

Gryson, Roger. *Le ministère des femmes dans l'église ancienne.* Gembloux, 1972.

Haegglund, Bengt. "Renaissance and Reformation." In *Luther and the Dawn of the Modern Era,* ed. Heiko A. Oberman, pp. 150–157. Leiden: E. J. Brill, 1974.

Harkness, Georgia E. *John Calvin: The Man and His Ethics.* New York: Abingdon Press, Apex Books, 1958.

Hefele, Karl Joseph von. *Histoire des conciles,* trans. Dom H. Leclercq. Paris, 1909. Vol. III.

Heideman, Eugene. *Reformed Bishops and Catholic Elders.* Grand Rapids: Wm. B. Eerdmans Publishing Co., 1970.

Hesselink, I. John. "Christ, the Law, and the Christian: An Unexplored Aspect of the Third Use of the Law in Calvin's Theology." In *Reformatio perennis: Essays on Calvin and the Reformation in Honor of Ford Lewis Battles,* ed. B. A. Gerrish with Robert Benedetto, pp. 11–26. Pittsburgh: Pickwick Press, 1981.

Hiemstra, William L. "Calvin's Doctrine of Christian Liberty." *Reformed Review* 13 (1959), pp. 10–14.

Irwin, Joyce. *Womanhood in Radical Protestantism: 1525–1675.* New York: Edwin Mellen Press, 1979.

Kelly, Joan. "Early Feminist Theory and the *Querelle des Femmes,* 1400–1789." *Signs* 8 (1982), pp. 4–28.

Kelly-Gadol, Joan. "Did Women Have a Renaissance?" In *Becoming Visible: Women in European History,* ed. Renate Bridenthal and Claudia Koonz, pp. 137–164. Boston: Houghton Mifflin Co., 1977.

Kelso, Ruth. *Doctrine for the Lady of the Renaissance.* Urbana: University of Illinois Press, 1956.

Kingdon, Robert M. *Geneva and the Consolidation of the French Protestant Movement 1564–1572: A Contribution to the History of Congregationalism, Presbyterianism, and Calvinist Resistance Theory.* Madison: University of Wisconsin Press, 1967.

Kraus, Hans-Joachim. "Calvin's Exegetical Principles." *Interpretation* 31 (1977), pp. 8–18.

Lehmann, Paul. "The Reformers' Use of the Bible." *Theology Today* 3 (1946), pp. 328–344.

Leith, John. *Introduction to the Reformed Tradition.* Atlanta: John Knox Press, 1977.

Littell, Franklin H. "New Light on Butzer's Significance." In *Reformation Studies: Essays in Honor of Roland H. Bainton,* ed. F. H. Littell, pp. 145–167. Richmond, Va.: John Knox Press, 1962.

Little, David. *Religion, Order, and Law: A Study in Pre-Revolutionary England.* New York: Harper & Row, 1969.

Maclean, Ian. *The Renaissance Notion of Woman: A Study in the Fortunes of Scholasticism and Medical Science in European Intellectual Life.* Cambridge:

Cambridge University Press, 1980.

Mancha, Rita. "The Woman's Authority: Calvin to Edwards." *The Journal of Christian Reconstruction* 6 (Winter 1979/80), pp. 86–98.

McCook, Henry Christopher. *Historic Decorations at the Pan-Presbyterian Council: A Photographic Souvenir.* Philadelphia, 1880; repr. Ottawa, 1982.

McDonnell,. Kilian, O.S.B. *John Calvin, the Church, and the Eucharist.* Princeton: Princeton University Press, 1967.

McKee, Elsie Anne. *John Calvin on the Diaconate and Liturgical Almsgiving.* Geneva: Librairie Droz, 1984.

McNeill, John T. "Calvin as an Ecumenical Churchman." *Church History* 32 (1963), pp. 379–391.

——— and James Hastings Nichols. *Ecumenical Testimony: The Concern for Christian Unity Within the Reformed and Presbyterian Churches.* Philadelphia: Westminster Press, 1974.

Mehl, Roger. *Catholic Ethics and Protestant Ethics.* Philadelphia: Westminster Press, 1971.

Meylan, Edward F. "The Stoic Doctrine of Indifferent Things and the Conception of Christian Liberty in Calvin's *Institutio religionis christianae.*" *Romanic Review* 28 (1937), pp. 135–145.

Midelfort, H. C. Eric. *Witch Hunting in Southwestern Germany 1562–1684: The Social and Intellectual Foundations.* Stanford: Stanford University Press, 1972.

Milner, Benjamin Charles. *Calvin's Doctrine of the Church.* Leiden: E. J. Brill, 1970.

Moeller, Bernd. *Imperial Cities and the Reformation: Three Essays,* ed. and trans. H. C. Eric Midelfort and Mark U. Edwards, Jr. Philadelphia: Fortress Press, 1972.

Monter, E. William. *Witchcraft in France and Switzerland: The Borderlands During the Reformation.* Ithaca: Cornell University Press, 1976.

———. "Pedestal and Stake: Courtly Love and Witchcraft." In *Becoming Visible: Women in European History,* ed. Renate Bridenthal and Claudia Koonz, pp. 119–136. Boston: Houghton Mifflin Co., 1977.

———. "Women in Calvinist Geneva (1550–1800)." *Signs: Journal of Women in Culture and Society* 6 (1980), pp. 189–209.

Naef, Henri. *Les origines de la Réforme à Genève.* Geneva, 1968.

Nauert, Charles G., Jr. *Agrippa and the Crisis of Renaissance Thought.* Urbana: University of Illinois Press, 1965.

Nijenhuis, Wilhelm. *Calvinus Oecumenicus: Calvin en de eenheid der kerk in het licht van zijn briefwisseling.* The Hague, 1958.

———. "Calvin and the Augsburg Confession." In *Ecclesia Reformata: Studies on the Reformation,* pp. 97–114. Leiden: E. J. Brill, 1972.

Oberman, Heiko A. *The Harvest of Medieval Theology: Gabriel Biel and Late Medieval Nominalism.* Cambridge, Mass.: Harvard University Press, 1963.

———. "Headwaters of the Reformation: Initia Lutheri—Initia Reformationis." In *Luther and the Dawn of the Modern Era,* ed. H. A. Oberman, pp. 40–88. Leiden: E. J. Brill, 1974.

————, ed. *Luther and the Dawn of the Modern Era*. Leiden: E. J. Brill, 1974.

Oberman, Heiko A., with Thomas A. Brady, Jr. *Itinerarium Italicum: The Profile of the Italian Renaissance in the Mirror of Its European Transformations*. Leiden: E. J. Brill, 1975.

Orth, Myra Dickman. "Francis Du Moulin and the *Journal* of Louise of Savoy." *Sixteenth Century Journal* 13 (1982), pp. 55–66.

Ozment, Steven E. *The Reformation in the Cities: The Appeal of Protestantism to Sixteenth-Century Germany and Switzerland*. New Haven: Yale University Press, 1975.

————. *The Age of Reform, 1250–1550: An Intellectual and Religious History of Late Medieval and Reformation Europe*. New Haven: Yale University Press, 1980.

————. *When Fathers Ruled: Family Life in Reformation Europe*. Cambridge, Mass.: Harvard University Press, 1983.

Parker, T. H. L. *Calvin's New Testament Commentaries*. Grand Rapids: Wm. B. Eerdmans Publishing Co., 1971.

————. *John Calvin: A Biography*. Philadelphia: Westminster Press, 1975.

Pater, Calvin A. *Karlstadt as the Father of the Baptist Movements*. Toronto: University of Toronto Press, 1984.

Pittard, Thérèse. *Femmes de Genève aux jours d'autrefois*. Geneva, n.d. (possibly 1946).

Quistorp, Heinrich. *Calvin's Doctrine of the Last Things*, trans. Harold Knight. Richmond, Va.: John Knox Press, 1955.

Richard, Lucien J. *The Spirituality of John Calvin: Its Sources and Originality*. Atlanta: John Knox Press, 1974.

Roelker, Nancy Lyman. *Queen of Navarre: Jeanne d'Albret, 1528–1572*. Cambridge, Mass.: Harvard University Press, 1968.

————. "The Appeal of Calvinism to French Noblewomen in the Sixteenth Century." *Journal of Interdisciplinary History* 2 (1972), pp. 391–418.

————. "The Role of Noblewomen in the French Reformation," *Archiv für Reformationsgeschichte* 63 (1972), pp. 168–195.

Ruether, Rosemary Radford, ed. *Religion and Sexism: Images of Woman in the Jewish and Christian Traditions*. New York: Simon & Schuster, 1974.

Russell, Jeffrey Burton. *Witchcraft in the Middle Ages*. Ithaca: Cornell University Press, 1972.

Schelkle, Karl Hermann. *Der Geist und die Braut. Die Frau in der Bibel*. Düsseldorf, 1977.

Sowards, J. K. "Erasmus and the Education of Women." *Sixteenth Century Journal* 13 (1982), pp. 77–89.

Steinmetz, David C. "Theological Reflections on the Reformation and the Status of Women." *Duke Divinity School Review* 41 (1976), pp. 197–207.

Street, Thomas Watson. "John Calvin on Adiaphora: An Exposition and Appraisal of His Theory and Practice." Th.D. dissertation, Union Theological Seminary, New York, 1954.

Telle, Émile. *L'oeuvre de Marguerite d'Angoulême, reine de Navarre, et la querelle des femmes*. Toulouse, 1937; repr. Geneva, 1969.

Tentler, Thomas N. *Sin and Confession on the Eve of the Reformation.* Princeton: Princeton University Press, 1977.

Torrance, Thomas F. *Calvin's Doctrine of Man.* London: Lutterworth Press, 1952.

————. *Kingdom and Church: A Study in the Theology of the Reformation.* Edinburgh: Oliver & Boyd, 1956.

Trinkaus, Charles. "Renaissance Problems in Calvin's Theology." In *Studies in the Renaissance*, ed. W. Peery, pp. 59–80. Austin: University of Texas, 1954.

Verkamp, Bernard J. *The Indifferent Mean: Adiaphorism in the English Reformation to 1554.* Athens, Ohio: Ohio University Press, 1977.

Wallace, Ronald S. *Calvin's Doctrine of the Christian Life.* Edinburgh: Oliver & Boyd, 1959.

Wendel, François. *Le mariage à Strasbourg á l'époque de la réforme, 1520–1692.* Strasbourg, 1928.

————. *L'église de Strasbourg: sa constitution et son organisation, 1532–1535.* Paris, 1942.

————. *Calvin: The Origins and Development of His Religious Thought,* trans. Philip Mairet. New York: Harper & Row, 1963.

Willis, E. David. "Rhetoric and Responsibility in Calvin's Theology." In *The Context of Contemporary Theology: Essays in Honor of Paul Lehmann*, ed. Alexander J. McKelway and E. David Willis, pp. 43–64. Atlanta: John Knox Press, 1974.

Woodward, William H. *Studies in Education During the Age of the Renaissance, 1400–1600.* New York: Russell & Russell, 1965.

Wyntjes, Sherrin Marshall. "Women in the Reformation Era." In *Becoming Visible: Women in European History*, ed. Renate Bridenthal and Claudia Koonz, pp. 165–191. Boston: Houghton Mifflin Co., 1977.

Index of Names